technical analysis

analysis

plain & simple

charting the markets in your language

MICHAEL N. KAHN

FINANCIAL TIMES

Prentice Hall

an imprint of Pearson Education

London · New York · San Francisco · Toronto · Sydney · Tokyo · Singapore
Hong Kong · Cape Town · Madrid · Paris · Milan · Munich · Amsterdam

PEARSON EDUCATION LIMITED

Head Office:
Edinburgh Gate
Harlow CM20 2JE
Tel: +44 (0) 1279 623623
Fax: +44 (0) 1279 431059

London Office:
128 Long Acre, London WC2E 9AN
Tel: +44 (0)171 447 2000
Fax: +44 (0)171 240 5771
www.business-minds.com

First published in Great Britain in 1999

© Pearson Education Limited 1999

The right of Michael N. Kahn to be identified as author
of this work has been asserted by him in accordance
with the Copyright, Designs and Patents Act 1988.

ISBN 0 273 63987 0

British Library Cataloguing in Publication Data
A CIP catalogue record for this book can be obtained from the British Library.

10 9 8 7

Typeset by Northern Phototypesetting Co. Ltd, Bolton.
Printed and bound in Great Britain by
Redwood Books, Trowbridge, Wiltshire.

The Publishers' policy is to use paper manufactured from sustainable forests.

About the author

Michael N. Kahn is chief technical analyst for BridgeNews, a division of Bridge Information Systems, a leading source of global financial information, transaction services, and network services.

Currently, Mr Kahn produces proprietary technical market commentary and analysis for distribution over both the customer network and the Internet. He also writes the monthly educational newsletter *Tips on Technicals* as well as regular articles for such publications as *SIMEX's Marketlink* and *Energy* magazines, *BridgeTrader* and *Technical Analysis of Stocks and Commodities* magazine. He is also a regular guest on the Nightly Business Report on PBS, has appeared on CNBC and is the Editor of the Market Technicians' Association newsletter *Technically Speaking*. His first book, *Real World Technical Analysis*, was published in January 1998 by Bridge/Commodity Research Bureau Publishing.

Prior to writing technical commentary, Mr Kahn was a senior product manager for Knight-Ridder Financial before that company was merged into Bridge. He was responsible for the marketing design of several of the firm's charting software platforms and launched technical analysis coverage for Knight-Ridder Financial News. He was also a co-editor of the *Tradecenter Market Letter*.

Prior to joining Bridge/Knight-Ridder Financial in 1986, Mr Kahn was a senior municipal bond specialist with Merrill Lynch. He also worked in the Financial Planning Department at Shearson Lehman American Express.

Mr Kahn holds a Bachelor of Arts in Physics and Economics from Brandeis University and a Master of Business Administration from New York University. He is also working on his Chartered Market Technician professional designation.

This book is dedicated to my father, Arthur M. Kahn
who would have loved to see it in print.

Contents

Preface

Technical analysis is one of the oldest market disciplines, yet the majority of the investment and academic communities consider it, at best, a minor supplement to their own work. At worst, it is disparaged as tea-leaf reading or simply a self-fulfilling prophecy. Look at these two phrases. They suggest that the technical analyst divines the market from some mystical process. This could not be further from the truth.

Consider the fundamental analyst. This person relies on company reports, conversations with company insiders and macro-economic research in relevant business sectors. All of this is indispensable when determining if a company is viable and predicting how its business will fare in future.

Now consider the source of all of the raw data. Much of it is projection and conjecture. How can you rely solely on such data when earnings reports and other industry-wide data will be subject to revisions?

Technical analysis looks at actual trades where bulls and bears have put their money where their collective mouths are. There is no revision of data. There is no ambiguity. There is no mystical divining of the future. All market and stock selection is based on current, not past, price performance, the predictable behaviour of market participants and the dynamics between markets over time.

Trends exist. Information is slowly disseminated to the public in an imperfect manner and as the public acts on the information, the markets move. They continue to move until either the last group has acted or an outside influence, such as news, ends the trend. Sounds a lot like physics, doesn't it? A body in motion tends to remain in motion.

Look at another aspect of the analysis. Behaviour is a key component of the analysis. When similar market conditions occur, market participants react in similar ways. This is how the patterns and measurements within technical analysis are created.

For example, the market holds fairly steady as buyers and sellers adjust their portfolios to meet their specific investment criteria. A stock might trade from 50 to 52 for weeks in this way. Is the stock good? Is the company good? You do not know. All you know is that bulls and bears consider the stock to be fairly valued within a small range. A body at rest tends to stay at rest – physics again.

Now, somebody comes into the market to buy a large block of stock. Why? Technical analysis does not know but more importantly, it does not care. All it needs to know is that money has flowed into the market and increased demand for the stock. Demand? That is straight from basic economics. If demand rises, the price must rise to induce sufficient supply (sellers) to come into the market and restore equilibrium. This doesn't sound very mystical, does it?

So, now that demand has increased, market activity picks up to provide supply. It also changes in character as people try to decipher what is happening. Here are the familiar concepts of fear and greed, both key determinants of human behaviour. Some participants will think that something has changed and the stock is now undervalued. It could be a new product or simply a decrease in the company's raw material inputs. Perhaps it is foreign capital coming into the stock. Or a shortage of stock itself. Whatever the reason, some market participants know something, or think they know something, about improved prospects for the company and they buy. The market breaks out of the trading range and as it does, more market participants act. The size and scope of their actions is most often similar to the size and scope of their actions at other occasions when the market has broken out of similar ranges. It can be measured and projected.

Technical analysis has an unfortunate name. Perhaps 'price action analysis' or 'supply, demand and reaction analysis' might be better. In 1998, great strides were made between market technicians and the academic community in the emerging field of behavioural finance. Now there is a possible name to use.

One aspect of the technical discipline is explaining the difference between valuations and actual market prices. If a stock is worth 75 on paper based on discounted cash flows, projected growth and overall economic conditions, why is it trading at 90? The difference is in the market's perceptions of the stock. People have pushed the stock up past its theoretical value and technical analysis is perfectly suited to handle this. Since people's perceptions can change quickly, it is also perfectly suited to reacting equally as quickly. This type of reaction speed is impossible using fundamental analysis alone.

So, do you scrap your fundamentals and rely exclusively on technicals? Absolutely not! While there are scores of money managers and traders that are 100 per cent technical and making a lot of money, you, the reader, are not interested in making technical analysis your sole investment discipline just yet. You are reading this book because you are seriously interested in enhancing your returns, not searching for a completely new method. Perhaps one day you will make that switch, but that is beyond the scope of this book.

At this stage, charts will give you a clear picture of what your fundamental research is saying. Remember that fundamentals describe the

> You are buying stock, not companies.

company. Technicals describe how the stock is performing. You are buying stock, not companies.

Acknowledgements

As with just about all books ever written, the author did not complete his work alone. This book is no exception.

First and foremost, I would like to thank my wife Susan for all she did to help bring this work to fruition. While it might be trite to thank a spouse who did none of the research nor write any of the words, Susan gave me a few things that were more valuable. She took on some of my responsibilities around the house and with the children to give me time to work in the evenings. Support for my vision and critiques for my output were also a necessity and on top of that, her gentle 'persuasion' to get the work done on time.

Next, I would like to thank the very professional staff at Financial Times Prentice Hall for first accepting my proposal and then dealing with me fairly and openly.

My friend, Mark Davidson, donated his time to proof read the text, not for spelling and grammar but to keep me focused on my intended audience. Debbie Stillman, I thank you for your help with the necessary legal details.

To Brian Goldstein, Marilyn Koretz, and, yes, my mother Natalie Kahn, who has been incredibly successful at picking stocks without knowing anything I wrote about in this book; thank you for letting me pick your brains.

As for non-individual investors, I would like to thank Bridge Information Systems for allowing me to use their charts and data here.

Finally, to my colleagues, both past and present, in the discipline of technical analysis, thank you for your pioneering work that served as the base for my own methods. There are some pretty smart people out there making their clients very wealthy and discovering some amazing secrets to pass along to their students.

About this book

Imagine that you speak only Mandarin and you want to read Shakespeare. Somebody has to translate it into your language. That is why this book was written. It will present technical analysis to you in your language and in the order that makes sense to you. You will go through the analytical process, calling on the tools as you need them, not as they might be organized in a textbook.

The author's career has been entirely within the financial services industry yet in most of my positions, I have served in the role as translator. I translated the research department's output into ideas for the sales force. I organized the trader's inventory into a solution for the brokerage customer. I spoke with customers and translated their needs into specifications to give to programmers and then translated the result back into learning aids for the sales force. This book is a logical extension of that. I hope to translate an often misunderstood, yet valuable, analytical discipline into simple tools any investor can put to immediate use. All of this can and will happen without compromising the quality of the analysis.

Core themes

Making money, not correct market forecasts

You need to be humble because the market is a lot bigger than you. You cannot tell the market what to do, even if it is 'wrong' by all measures. It can hold a 'losing' position a lot longer than you or even your country's central bank can. What you want to do is listen to the market. It will tell you where it is going, so you can jump on for the ride.

With technical analysis, the worst case is a bad trade from a false breakout. Humility allows you to acknowledge your error immediately and cut your losses.

At its best, technical analysis will never let you miss a big move. That does not include the unusual situations of legal changes, buyouts or natural disasters. However, if a market is going to have a sustained move either down or up, technical analysis will get you out or keep you in respectively. It probably will not be at the very beginning or the very end, but you will capture the bulk of the move and get out before giving back a significant portion of your profits.

What makes a stock look good?

To be trite, a stock that is going to go up is the one that looks good. Why state it like this? The answer is that you should not be interested in only flashy, glamour stocks or common household names. You need to look for stocks where demand exceeds supply, where the so-called smart money has been placed in the early stages of their individual bull markets. Stocks that are already moving higher with increasing public interest are ideal candidates. These are all evident on price charts with supporting indicators.

A rising tide raises most boats.

Notice that there is no mention of companies with solid fundamentals. Strong balance sheets and good earnings growth make for good companies. On paper, this suggests a certain price range over time.

In the real world, valuations are only one component of stock prices. Investor perceptions of value, based on supply and demand, economics, politics, pop culture and fear and greed make up the difference between fundamental valuation and market price. Price can be higher or lower than valuation. Technical analysis seeks to follow price trends, not paper valuations.

What makes a stock look good? Find at least three of the following and chances are, you will pick a winner:

- A rising price trend as more and more investors jump aboard;
- Rising volume as investors become more aggressive in their purchases;
- Strong, but not excessive, price momentum. Anything higher indicates that supply and demand are out of synch;
- A strong sector. If the sector is doing well, there is likely to be enough business for all the stocks in it;
- Strong market. A rising tide raises most boats;
- Supportive environment. Low input prices, high output prices, low cost of doing business, favourable supply and demand in the industry.

All of this information is available on the charts. Supportive environment sounds like fundamental analysis and it is to a degree. Technicians call this intermarket analysis. For example, an electric utility has high energy input costs and is often saddled with a good deal of debt. A bear market in oil and gas combined with a rally in the bond market (declining interest rates) suggests favourable conditions for the stock.

Choosing the right tools

Technical analysis offers a vast array of tools for every type of analytical task. There are charts that display prices in time frames ranging from trade-by-trade to daily to monthly and longer. They can show market cycles, phases of fear and greed and projected targets.

Indicators are available to measure price momentum, volume distribution and market breadth. There are even methods in popular use to measure sentiment and how perceptions change. For the purposes of this book you will stick to the basics and use those tools available to the individual investor.

Flexible analysis for the real world

Allow yourself to *hear* what the market is telling you and be able to listen to it, no matter what you may have thought beforehand. *See* patterns develop. *Feel* the changing tides of investor sentiment. If you need further sensory reinforcement, *smell* your profits and *taste* success.

Strict interpretation of technical rules is, of course, the best way to learn the topic, but this book will focus more on the spirit of the law instead. This will allow you to take the concepts as you need them, rather than follow a textbook outline.

What this book is about

This book was designed to do three things: enhance your returns, help you avoid bad trades and get you to think in terms of probabilities.

Enhancing your returns

Even this early, it is important to repeat the point that at this stage in your investment career, technical analysis will not and should not replace other methods. You should focus on enhancing your other decision-making processes to increase the likelihood of success. You will expand your set of investment decision-making tools and learn to select the right tool for the job.

The following chapters also take the mystery out of technical analysis. The entity called 'the market' is really made of the collective actions of human beings. It can therefore be analyzed with tools that measure crowd behaviour and the imperfect dissemination of information. Sounds hard? It is not. A chart with supporting indicators can do this with relative ease.

Finally, there is a visual (sensory) component to the numbers (earnings, sales, etc.). In the investment world, a picture really is worth a thousand words.

Avoiding bad trades

If enhancing your returns deals with buying the best stocks then avoiding bad trades is just another way to express that thought. Technical analysis can quickly show you situations where the stock has drifted too far away from its fundamental value and is therefore not presenting a good opportunity. It can also tell you that a stock is not healthy when it fails to react to what should have been good news (higher earnings, new product, better business environment). If the stock does not rally on good news, it may mean that the bulls are exhausted. They may have already bought their share and therefore do not demand any more.

Probabilities

Technical analysis is about probabilities and escapes. People probably react in similar fashion to similar situations but it is not guaranteed. Proper analysis will give you the probability of a correct buy or sell decision as well as tell you right away when you have made a mistake.

Even if your analysis and decision were absolutely correct, the world changes. When it does, the technical condition of the stock or market changes. The charts will alert you that you need to reevaluate your positions.

What this book is not about

Do not worry that you might read about sophisticated analysis and therefore think like a short-term trader at the stock exchange. Treatment of each subject is kept deliberately light.

You will not have to wade through a discourse on how the market works or how to manage your personal finances. It is assumed that you already know this. This book is not concerned with why you are investing, other than to make money.

Finally, there will be no discussion of earnings, sales, revenues, debt, weather, harvests or other fundamental data other than to mention that fundamentals do drive the stock price in the long term. Respect them but do not use them directly in the stock-picking decision.

How to get the most from this book

This book is aimed at serious individual investors seeking to augment their current stock picking abilities. It is also of value to the professional investor or trader in any market (stock, bond, currency or commodity) who has not yet used technical analysis and is seeking additional tools for decision making. Whether you are investing alone or as part of an investment club, this book will explain the basics of chart reading, market timing and even some money management.

Read the first section to get an overall feel for what technical analysis is all about. Then, take one chapter at a time and see how it applies to what you are already doing. Examine some of your past trades that worked out well to see if the technical condition present was favourable. Next, look at some of your past trades that did not work out, to see if technical analysis could have kept you away from them or at least told you quickly, before too much money was lost, that they had gone bad.

Do not rely exclusively on what you learn here. Technical analysis is both an art and a science in that it can be rigorously tested but it still depends on the experience of the analyst to set parameters of precision and risk tolerance. Again, use the concepts presented here to augment your current analysis. There will be time later to study the topic in detail, so for now, your job is to increase your investment returns right away.

You don't have to abandon the fundamentals

We will be focusing on supplementing your current stock selection discipline, so you will not have to give up your broker's advice, advisory services or favourite hot tips. Rather, you will learn how to evaluate these recommendations, to see if they are technically sound and therefore be able to determine if the time is right for the investment. You will also be able to track your current portfolio to find advance warnings of impending reversal. In other words, you will be able to keep more of your profits because you will be able to sell quickly and with more confidence.

If your broker calls with a new recommendation, consider delaying a purchase when the chart looks bad. The market is telling you something that has not yet appeared in the fundamentals. Remember that if nobody is buying the stock, no matter what the fundamentals say, it will not go up. Also, markets can trade far away from their underlying fundamental values and technical analysis will tell you when that is happening. In the stock market, a company may be very profitable and a leader in a growing industry but its stock may have traded to unrealistic levels. The company is great. The stock is not.

Technical analysis is portable

We may talk a lot about stocks but almost everything here is relevant in the bond, currency and commodity markets. Chart patterns and trends are valid in all markets. Some instructors actually take well-known indices, multiply their values by a constant and then turn the chart upside down when they present it to their classes. The analysis is nearly identical to the unaltered chart.

Yes, it is true that markets act somewhat differently at tops than they do at bottoms. It is also true that each market and individual stock has its own 'personality'. However, for our purposes in basic analysis, the nuances and subtleties can be ignored.

Daily charts are used where each unit summarizes the trading activity of a single day, but almost everything you will learn is valid in all time frames. Daily charts are great for 3–9 month analysis. Longer time horizons require weekly or monthly charts where each chart unit summarizes a week or month, respectively, of trading data. If you are a short-term trader, charts in the hourly or minute time frames are needed. However, learning to day-trade is not why you are reading this book.

Finally, since technical tools work in most markets, you can cover more ground than a fundamental analyst. That means you will be able to analyze a technology company, food retailer and a bank with equal ease. You will even be able to chart interest rates and oil prices to help with your stock selection.

You may be less detailed but you are not using only one analytical method. Your goal is profits, not analytical expertise. Let the business media interview the expert. You are here to make money.

part 1

A few things you'll need to know before you begin

1 Required background

As much as it would be good to jump right into learning technical analysis, it is still a good idea to understand some broad concepts.

The past

'Those who cannot remember the past are condemned to repeat it.'
George Santayana

Historical data

When investment professionals as a group make their decisions, they often analyze such fundamental information as economics, politics and demographics. They look back to the past to forecast what may happen in the future. This does not mean that they are consulting a magic oracle but rather, they are employing technical analysis of the markets. This discipline relies on generous amounts of historical price data that is both accurate and readily available to their computer applications.

> Investors and speculators react the same way to the same types of events.

Technical analysis is based on human behaviour, but it is not a study in psychology. Investors and speculators react the same way to the same types of events again and again and this is reflected in the ebb and flow of prices. If one charts this activity over time, patterns in the price action emerge. Some of these patterns comprise standard technical analysis, while others are created by analysts based on their own observations and calculations. Historical data are required in both cases to test theories and fine tune their parameters.

When currency traders, for example, are deciding whether or not to buy yen they may look at a chart of yen prices for the past year to determine if the recent rally has ended. This graphical representation makes it a quick study. By expanding the chart to cover more years, they can quickly find other occasions when the yen rose quickly and what happened just after it did.

History repeats

Technical price patterns are often followed by similar reactions. For example, if prices were rising and then start to trade in a small range, the characteristics (shape and size) of the range can be used to determine how far the market will move once the pattern is ended. This is not just a guess, but a highly likely condition (reaction by humans) based on thousands of similar occurrences in the past. The more historical data the investor has available, the more historical observations can be made and the more likely the investor will make a correct buy or sell decision.

The biggest advantage to using a historical database in making these decisions is that it gives the trader or analyst perspective. A sharp price increase in one commodity today may be taken as a bullish sign until it is viewed as part of a longer chart that has been declining for the past six months. In that light, the rally in a commodity may well be an opportunity to unload it rather than load up on it.

One of the biggest criticisms is that technical analysis is a self-fulfilling prophecy. Wearing a 'making money, not forecasts' hat sounds like a good deal for those who get in early. Stepping back from the profits for a moment, it should be conceded that the criticism is true in some cases.

One definition of a technical breakout says that a market that moves above the top of a technical pattern should be bought. Short-term traders who see this buy and the market moves higher due to increased demand.

This works well on the initial breakout as new buyers are drawn in. However, unless there are more technical factors supporting the move, the rally will fail. In this case, the prophecy will not come true. For a sustained rally, there must be increasing demand and increasing participation from the public (individual or institutional). True breakouts are usually presaged by changes in the underlying technical condition, have certain confirming characteristics at the breakout and are followed by improving technical indications.

Although this undermines the self-fulfilling prophecy argument, rallies, chart patterns and breakouts can all be measured and followed because people do repeat their actions. A triangle in today's market is formed for many of the same reasons that it was formed before. A breakout now will probably create the same result.

History repeats itself in the same way that snow flakes look alike. From a distance, they look the same. When put under the microscope, the differences become apparent. In the markets, human participants tend to do the similar things given similar circumstances. For example, if a rally stalls and a triangle pattern forms on the charts, buyers and sellers become increasingly uncertain about what to do. They buy and sell with less confidence as they wait for some outside influence to spark the next move, higher or lower. The fact that there are at least five different variations of triangles tells us that these periods of increasing uncertainty are not exactly alike.

What does a budding technician make of all this? Following the basic rules of market behaviour will be profitable most of the time and we must be nimble enough to react when events deviate from the expected.

This summarizes the similarity of market actions without locking us into strict definitions. People tend to do similar things given similar conditions. We learn from our mistakes. However, there are always new people entering the market that have not yet had their lessons.

Repetition and rhyming

Are no two snowflakes exactly alike? Does lightning ever strike twice? Does a bull market last the same time and move the same distance?

It was Mark Twain who said 'History does not repeat itself. But it does rhyme.' No matter how much today's market may look like a previous market, you cannot be 100 per cent sure it will continue to react in the same way. It may go up, but not as fast. It may pause to rest in a quiet trading range, or it may pause to rest in a volatile trading range.

With so many variables that can affect the market, the difference between having 80 and 90 per cent of them in line probably does not matter to a bottom-line decision of buy, sell or hold. It might affect the course or amount of the rally, but not the decision the investor makes to buy or sell.

Technical market theory

Most people know little about how the car works but they know how to drive it and when to take it in for service. Technical market theory encompasses a large body of work, rigorous testing and decades of experience. At this stage all of that is much more than we need to get started, but we do need to know how to use the 'key' and start up.

As technical investors we are chart readers. The key is to think of a chart in psychological, not graphic terms. In other words, support is the level at which the aggressive selling of the bears has waned sufficiently to be offset by the rising aggressiveness of buying by the bulls. Resistance is the level at which the aggressive buying of the bulls has waned sufficiently to be offset by the rising aggressiveness of selling by the bears.

The basics of technical analysis

Chart patterns represent the behaviour of the masses. They are built from actual transactions, so in effect, they represent how the pool of investors, traders, speculators and hedgers have put their money where their collective mouths were over time.

Since the composition of the pool stays relatively stable over time and investors react the same way time and time again when presented with the same circumstances, chart patterns can be used to measure the likelihood of similar resolutions to current market conditions in the future.

Since not all players have access to the same information at the same time and they do not react at the same speed when they do get it, markets present opportunity. If everyone knew about a new product announcement from the Widget Company

> Not all players have access to the same information at the same time.

at the same time and they reacted the same way, the stock would only trade at the market maker's bid-ask spread until the news came out. It would then jump completely to the next level, where it would trade perfectly flatly until the next news development. Trends represent the slow dissemination and assimilation of news.

Since the market really consists of the mass of human will, it is prone to excessive swings from optimism to pessimism and back again. Technical analysis helps to measure these swings.

Humans again – market psychology

This emerging field of analysis is beyond the scope of this book. However, a few of the basic concepts can be learnt, that directly apply to analyzing a stock or market and a few that are indirectly indicated in the charts.

Perceptions

It is worth reiterating that a stock's price often does not match its fundamental value. Current market price can and does deviate from the (forgive the jargon) capital asset price model and discounted value of future cash flows. In a marketplace where humans, not computers, determine prices, it is not what it is worth, it is what people think it is worth.

How else can the phenomenon of Internet stocks be explained? In 1998 and 1999, these stocks tripled after their initial public offerings when they had no profits and unreliable revenues. And the 1987 crash? How can the fundamental value of the entire stock market be cut by almost one-third in one day when there was little change elsewhere outside the investment world?

Leading into the crash, people were ignoring such important factors as soaring interest rates and the prevalence of a 'buy anything' mentality. When reality caught up with perceptions, prices tumbled.

To rephrase this, the stock market or any other market never reflects cal-culated true value. It reflects people's perception of the value; what people think it is worth.

The crowd vs the individual

People like to believe that they are independent thinkers and that rational analysis and logic often prevail. They also might be modest enough to admit that other people have valid, and even superior, opinions.

When those same, rationally thinking people are part of a crowd, they tend to conform to the crowd. It is uncomfortable to maintain a minority opinion, even when the individual's analysis is sound. As part of a crowd, humility is lost, as everyone begins to think that they (the crowd) are 100 per cent right. There is no room for contrary opinion. Facts not confirming the mass opinion are ignored.

In the previous section, the 1987 crash was used as an example. The crowd wanted to buy stocks and the market went up. The rare dissenter was called a 'doomsayer' even though the evidence for a crash was in place.

The same condition is in effect at market bottoms. The crowd sees noth-ing but bad news and the market continues to fall. Changing conditions are ignored as they were in 1982, even as the dawn of the greatest bull market of all time was at hand.

Technical analysts have the tools to follow the changing tide. Confidence in their analysis provides the conviction to act as an individual, against the crowd, if necessary.

Myths and truths

A few of the myths surrounding technical analysis have been covered: the self-fulfilling prophecy, basing future price activity on past performance, reading tea leaves have been convered. There can be some truth to self-ful-filling prophecy. After a stock breaks higher from a chart pattern, new buy-ers are drawn in. They push the price higher and that, in turn, draws in still more buyers.

The problem with this explanation is that it unknowingly merges short- and long-term analysis with a once-time action (breakout) into one story. Short-term analysis would have told short-term traders to buy before the breakout. If technical conditions continue to improve after the breakout, then long-term analysis would confirm it with improved momentum (prices move convincingly) and higher volume (more shares change hands suggesting broader public participation). Investor sentiment would improve as the changes in fundamental data filtered down to all investors.

The past-performance issue is another of the critics' favourites. How can past performance determine the future? The 'random walk' theory of markets says that if prices are random then nothing can predict them. But prices are not random. Prices are based on calculated value modified higher or lower by human perceptions of value. Calculated value changes in predictable ways based on the economy and the individual company.

How perceptions will change cannot be calculated but they can be measured based on current buying and selling in the market. Buying and selling leave measurable footprints on the charts and since humans tend to do the similar things given similar circumstances, it can be forecasted what the market, as the sum of all humans participating, will do next.

It is not the past action of stocks that are used to predict the future. Rather, it is the form and extent of current trading and the time-tested knowledge of what people have done after similar patterns in the past that determines supply and demand. This allows prices to be forecast.

For fundamentalists

'The biggest mistake that a fundamental analyst makes is thinking that a stock and a company are the same thing. The biggest mistake a technician makes is thinking that a stock and a company are different.' – Phil Roth, chief technical market analyst, Morgan Stanley Dean Witter.

Even the most ardent believer in fundamental analysis could benefit from technical analysis. Technical analysis helps to time purchases and sales of securities. When a company receives glowing fundamental reports, its stock may not be good to buy. It may have already run up on the news or anticipation of the news. It may have been caught in a frenzy of activity that was unrelated to the fundamentals. Internet stocks were a good example of this.

Technical analysis helps to determine if the price of the stock has moved to an extreme. Price in the market can and does become decoupled from the fundamentals.

Even a fundamental analyst in technical denial uses some technical information, such as 52-week price range and earnings history. The former represents a crude measure of past performance. The latter is actually the trend in earnings.

To recap, this book is not about getting you to abandon your fundamentals. It is about enhancing your analysis with charts. This author is a fully-fledged technician, but you do not have to be.

What is technical analysis?

What a terrible name has been bestowed upon this method of market analysis – technical. It is about as technical as singing. Designing electronic circuit boards is technical. Developing a new bio-medical implant device is technical. Market analysis? That is not technical.

True, there are technical terms and complicated research. Mathematical modelling can also play a role but strip away all the advanced level components, and technical analysis is just a tool investors and traders use when deciding to buy or sell a stock, bond, currency or commodity.

One analogy that can be used is that of the carpenter. Market technicians carry with them a technical toolbox filled with the studies, patterns and classifications. The carpenter uses a hammer to drive a nail, not a screwdriver. The technical analyst might use a momentum indicator to assess the health of the market, not linear regression. Both tools are good but each has its own special use.

Technical analysts do not even expect to be correct in their decisions all the time. With the proper money management and mastery of one's ego, a 60 per cent success rate will put one at the head of the class. A little higher success rate would be expected from a doctor or an airport control tower. Perfection is technical. Market analysis is not.

So how is technical analysis like singing? For starters, everyone can do it. Most people may not be good at it and therefore will not be doing concerts for the Queen. Others, with training, practice and desire, will master the basics to make their portfolios sing.

Sure, singing can be broken down into physiological components of breathing, posture, and throat control. Psychologists may cite right brain dominance and perhaps innate musical ability. Most singers, save for those at the top professional levels, do not study these components. Rather, they know the basics of singing and apply it for fun. This is the feeling you should get from this book as you learn a few lessons in market analysis. You do not need to know every study and every technique top technical traders use, because you are not trying to become a top technical trader at this point in your investing career. You will have your 'fun' when you see your results improve. Maybe you will get hooked on charts and decide to pursue technical analysis as your primary discipline. Maybe not. You are not going to change from a karaoke singer to Frank Sinatra overnight.

Technical analysis has been saddled with a poorly descriptive name. Technical analysis is not technical like electronics, but more diagnostic like the role of a doctor.

Components

Technical analysis is the art of identifying market turning points at a relatively early stage. The goal for all but the most aggressive of traders is to ride the bulk of the trend as far as possible without attempting to pick the exact tops and bottoms.

The chart

The basic component of technical analysis is the chart. Depending on how detailed the analysis is going to be, the chart captures all relevant data and displays it in a logical format. Of all the information that can emerge from it, the most important is *how* the market got to where it is at any given point in time. How it moved from price A to price B over time reveals a great deal about supply and demand, investor sentiment and pent-up price potential.

> The basic component of technical analysis is the chart.

Consider a market that has moved in a very small price range for months. Trading activity has been relatively low and very little news has emerged. In short, the market is boring. Few people are interested in following it at all. One day, trading volume suddenly doubles. Given that low normal volume, this doubling is still mostly unnoticed by the public but the people who bought that day knew something was going on. Perhaps they only thought they knew something but the result is the same, a doubling of volume.

For whatever reason, demand rises. The market breaks out of its price range, something technicians call a base or basing pattern, and begins to rise. Often, the good news that caused this breakout is released to the public and the rally begins in earnest.

Is this inside information? No, it is not. Remember that information flow is not perfect. Somebody either knew it early or took a gamble that is was true. If information flowed to everyone at the same time then there would be no such thing as a bull or bear market. Prices would jump from one equilibrium level to the next in an instant. Technical analysis attempts to determine where the market is in the process of information dissemination to determine if it is in the early, middle or late stages of a trend.

The supporting cast

To the basic chart can be added indicators that quantify market momentum (how fast the market is moving), trade volume (how much power is behind the moves) and even the natural order of crowd behaviour (sentiment).

A complete technical analysis of a stock, for example, could also include technical treatment of fundamental data such as earnings and dividends. To say that company XYZ has raised its dividend for 20 quarters in a row is to say that the trend in dividends is rising at a steady rate. A plot of earnings that shows an increasing slope suggests that stock prices will soon follow.

Discussion of studies will be kept to a minimum in this book. Its goal is to expand your decision-making skills, not teach the complete set of technical tools. There are many good specialist texts to help you with that task.

What is the market?

Just as is learned in Introduction to Economics courses, the market for stocks, bonds, commodities or foreign exchange is comprised of buyers and sellers. The price at which they trade is determined by supply and demand.

The list below breaks the process down further. As can be seen, the prime mover of markets is the perceptions of the people in it.

- The market is comprised of buyers and sellers
- Price is determined by supply and demand
- Supply and demand are determined by the aggressiveness of the bulls and the bears
- Bullish and bearish actions arise from perceptions of value.

Notice that actual value is not in the list. What a market *should* be worth based on mathematical and economic models is not the deciding factor in the prices in the morning newspaper tables. Technical analysis is positioned to follow the discrepancies between forecast and perceived value.

The herd

The psychology of crowds, also known as the herd mentality, is an important part of technical analysis. Why the herd? Investors and traders are also human beings. Humans prefer to be accepted in their herds and like their animal counterparts, they will follow the herd for psychological safety.

Continuing with the animal analogy, imagine a herd of zebras in Africa perceives a threat from a nearby pride of lions. The herd begins to run. All zebras within it stay together to present a blur of white and black stripes to the lions. This is a trend. As long as the herd moves, all individual zebras will move with it and consider themselves safe. Consider this the zoological equivalent of the 'trend is your friend', one of the more common adages in the investment world.

Now imagine that the herd becomes so preoccupied with the simple act of running that it forgets to look ahead at the changing landscape. Up ahead is a deep ravine. Here, at the end, the trend is no longer your friend so to avoid certain death, the individual zebra should be looking for a way to break from the herd. This is a lonely proposition for both zebra and investor – going against the crowd to stand alone. The zebra must consider if the lion is still out there. The investor must weigh the psychological discomfort of standing alone against the financial discomfort of following the crowd past the end of the rally.

So what is the market? It is the conglomeration of the actions and perceptions of all participants. It develops its own consciousness, not unlike that of millions of nerve cells coming alive together in a brain. Like a living organism, no single cell is more important than the whole so we, as individual cells, must remember our place. The market can never be wrong.

What is a chart?

Charts are everywhere. We use them to keep tabs on how our children are growing, how to group ourselves demographically and what the weather is going to be for the next five days. Whenever we show how something changes over time or how it breaks down into its component parts, we are using charts. In the investment world, we usually chart price movements over time. Technical analysis starts with this basic chart.

A picture is worth a thousand words

Technical analysis is based on the premise that in order to know where prices are going, one must know where prices have been. In the early days of stock trading, the only way to know where prices had been was to read the ticker tape. Only a very few had access to the tape.

Since most of us are not working on the floor of the exchange, computers read the tape and send the prices to home screens and newspapers. However, even getting an idea of the market from these quotes is nearly impossible. The more stocks (or mutual funds, bonds, and futures) are followed, the harder it is to do investment research. Only so much information can be kept track of in one's head.

Enter the chart. By plotting the closing prices of stocks or other instruments on paper (or a computer screen) each day it can be seen at a glance not only what the price of the stock is but how it got there. Sure, MicroGiant is trading at 65 up ½ but was it 60 last week or 70? Charts put all the data in one place so they can be visually assimilated at will.

What good is that?

Knowing if a market is moving up or down helps investors to buy only those issues that have the odds stacked in their favour. The bottom line in all markets, whether they be financial, real estate or breakfast cereal, is that when demand is greater than supply, prices will rise. A chart with a positively-sloped price line is exhibiting excess demand. It is better to buy a stock when demand is greater than supply than the other way around.

The chart of Micron Technology for 1995 and early 1996 illustrates this. On the way up, when all the news was positive, buying high and selling higher was a good strategy. In late 1995, when the price had fallen 25 points, the chart shows prices bouncing back a bit. Certainly, if the stock was good at 90, it is a steal at 70. It wasn't even a steal when it dropped to 50.

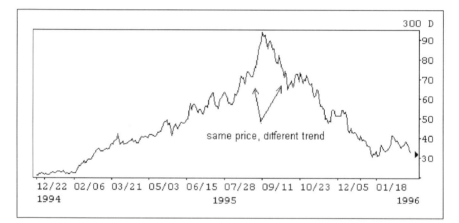

Fig 3.1 ■ Micron Technology

Technical analysis has many tools that it can apply to charts. Many of them are esoteric or proprietary and never make it to the mainstream. Of those that are generally available, the majority are used infrequently. Any investor can be armed with a small number of technical tools and be able to enhance their performance in the markets. The goal is not to be the best investor there ever was. The goal is to enhance portfolio returns in a way that is consistent with an individual's needs and risk profile.

The goal is not to be the best investor there ever was.

Tea leaves? Crystal ball?

Want to insult a market technician? Ask what is seen in the crystal ball. Technical analysis cannot see into the future any more than can reading the bumps on your head. It does not predict. It is more about crowd psychology and probability. Charts simply show the current situation. The analysis lays out the probabilities for various possible outcomes.

The catchphrase for technicians has always been 'history repeats.' The latest revision of this phase is 'history doesn't repeat, it rhymes.' Events do not unfold the same way every time but the odds of similar paths are quite high.

Applying one simple tool to Figure 3.1 a simple trendline (essentially a stick figure drawing of the stock's price action) was broken to the downside in November 1995. History tells you that when this happens, the likely event is for the market to keep going in the direction of the break. Anybody who thought they got a good deal at 70 a month earlier was told very clearly that they were wrong.

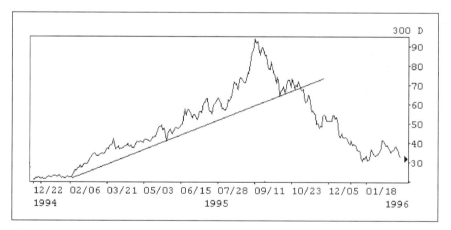

Fig 3.2 ■ Micron Technology 2

Technical analysis is not always right. Nothing is. Every technical tool in the world can agree that Joe's Customized Research Company is a stock on the verge of its great bull market when a little thing like the Internet comes along to change the rules of the game. Technical analysis will quickly point out that the original forecast was wrong. In the investment world, being wrong 60 per cent of the time still makes us very wealthy.

Of course, losing 60 per cent of the time with even-money odds is a bad game. Technical analysis requires the investor to follow the age-old adage of cutting losses and letting profits ride. Four $10 winners swamp six $1 losers. This is how traders make serious money. Long-term investors should really shoot for portfolio enhancement rather than aggressive activity, but the key is that they should not be afraid of a loss. A disciplined investing approach will not be sidetracked by them in the long run.

What about earnings?

There is no doubt that what a company earns has a direct impact on its value. Technical analysis does not consider earnings, financial statements, news and input prices directly. Rather, it assumes that all of that information is in the current price. A better definition is that price is the sum total to date of the actions of everyone in the marketplace. Somebody was following earnings and bought or sold the stock. Someone else was watching the news wires to find developments affecting the company. Input prices are followed by others. If the price of apples and wheat flour go up, the margins at Aunt Betty's Fruit Pie Company will be squeezed. This is technical analysis.

In the credit markets, there is always the fundamental argument that interest rates are affected by the actions of the Federal Reserve Bank and changes in inflation. The statement that the Fed has lowered the discount rate for the past six quarters means that the discount rate chart is trending down. What happens when the consumer price index rises? This, too, can be charted and both correlated to interest rates. A chart of interest rates themselves captures the actions of those following these supposedly fundamental data. Most investors are using technical analysis already without even knowing it.

Conclusion

Charts are not mysterious. They are tools that allow investors to keep track of more opportunities and see quickly when it is time to change strategies. They do not predict the future but they are valuable in determining the probabilities of success for the decision to buy, sell or hold.

Jargon you cannot avoid

Here is the bare minimum of technical terms and concepts.

Bar chart

The bar chart is the main market analysis tool in the western world and a key component of technical analysis worldwide. In east Asian countries, a form of charting called 'candle charting' is the major tool but the data series they both use are the same. Candle charts are covered in their own chapter at the end of this book.

Daily bars use open, high, low and close data to summarize trading activity for a single day. They are plotted together in a vertical line each day as can be seen in Figure 4.1. Over time, the bars rise and fall to form the chart patterns that will be explained later.

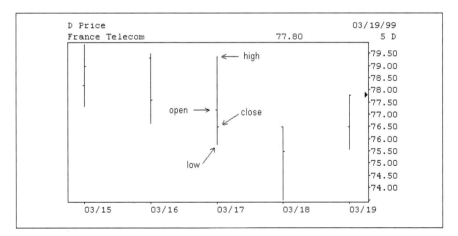

Fig 4.1 ■ Five-day bar chart of France Telecom

Figure 4.1 shows a five-day bar chart of France Telecom. The high and low prices are connected to form the body of the bar. The open is the small tick mark on the left side of the bar. The close is the tick mark on the right side of the bar.

Support and resistance

Simply stated, support and resistance are respective price levels at which price stops going down or up. A price in any market is one at which bulls and bears have agreed upon fair value. If bulls think that the price is low, they will attempt to buy. This, in turn, raises demand and prices rise. As prices rise, bulls become less aggressive in their actions and bears become more aggressive. At some point, bullish and bearish aggressiveness will balance and that price level becomes resistance.

The converse is true for support as the aggressiveness of the bears falls while the aggressiveness of the bulls rises. When they balance, prices stop falling and support is established.

Notice that aggressiveness balances. Supply and demand are always in balance at any given price because a trade price was agreed upon. Because the markets have memory of previous support and resistance levels, they can be used as target or limit prices when the markets have traded away from them. In other words, if a rally ended a year ago, the top of the rally becomes resistance for the next rally attempt. The market remembers that bulls and bears were in equilibrium there. Perhaps current traders and investors remember it that way. Perhaps that price level is a trigger for some economic event that stops the rally such as a certain price in crude oil triggering new exploration and hence greater oil supply.

Chart patterns are bound by support and resistance. Trendlines are support and resistance lines on an angle.

Figure 4.2 shows a 6½ year trading range for the Nikkei index in Japan. The same levels served as support and resistance there for years.

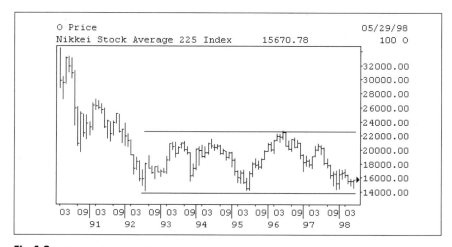

Fig 4.2 ■ Year trading range for the Nikkei index in Japan

Trends

The theory underlying these indicators is that once a trend is in motion, it will continue in that direction. Technical analysis attempts to determine the strength and the direction of the trend. The earlier that this can be accomplished, the earlier the trend can be followed and the more profit can be made. Knowing the trend is equally as important as avoiding bad trades. Strategies such as buying the dips work well if the trend is going your way. If it is not, the risk is higher and the potential profit is smaller.

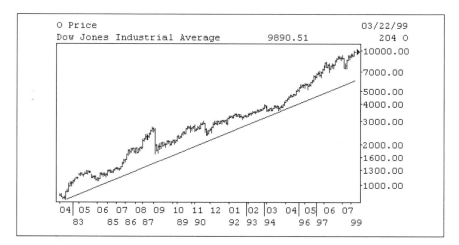

Fig 4.3 ■ Long-term trend for Dow-Jones Industrial Average

Figure 4.3 shows how long trends can last. The long-term trend for the Dow-Jones Industrial Average is unbroken for the 16 years leading into the publication of this book. Shorter-term trends came and went but the long-term trend remained intact.

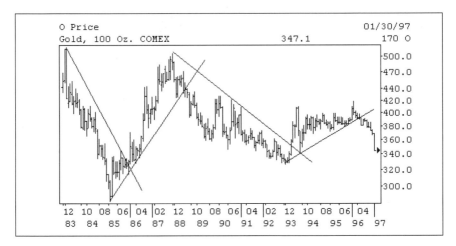

Fig 4.4 ■ Multi-year trends in gold

Figure 4.4 shows multi-year trends in gold. Trendlines work in all time frames and in all markets.

Consolidation, congestion, correction

All of these terms describe the same event in the markets. After a rally, a certain portion of the bulls decide that prices are above fair value. They take advantage by locking in these excess profits with a sale. At the same time, even the most timid of the bears decides that the market is just too attractive not to sell short (selling short is a bearish strategy to sell borrowed stock or futures now and buy them back later). This combination changes the balance in the market, increases supply and prices fall.

During this decline, portfolios are realigned, news is digested and investors enter and leave the market. The way all of this unfolds determines the shape of the pattern on the chart. Consolidation and congestion are terms that can be applied to any time frame, from minute to daily to monthly. Correction seems to be a relative term, since a correction in a long-term trend may be considered an outright bear market in the short term.

The bottom line for this section is that any market that is not trending higher or lower can probably be labelled with one of these terms.

This is covered in more detail in Chapters 5 to 11 on chart patterns.

Breakout

After a market forms a pattern, it eventually starts a new trend higher or lower. A breakout occurs when prices move through either the supporting or resisting border of a chart pattern. News or market events cause the perceptions of the bulls and bears to change and one or the other becomes more aggressive in their activities. If it is the bulls, then the market goes up. If it is the bears, then the market goes down.

> A breakout occurs when prices move through either the supporting or resisting border of a chart pattern.

Breakouts occur with sudden shifts in perception that causes increased activity from an increased number of market participants. Volume usually rises and prices usually move in wider intraday ranges.

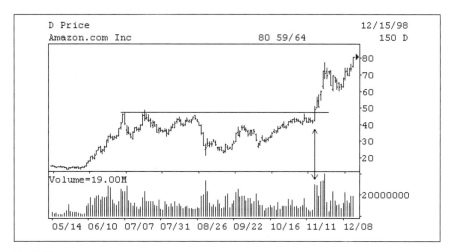

Fig 4.5 ■ Breakouts

Breakouts are covered in Chapter 14.

Continuation patterns

A continuation pattern is a consolidation zone that serves as a rest stop during a trend. After bulls and bears reevaluate their positions and portfolios, the market continues on with the existing trend. Whichever group was the more aggressive before the pattern resumes this leadership.

This is covered in detail in Chapter 8.

Reversal patterns

A reversal pattern is a consolidation zone that serves as a rest stop when the trend is changing. Bulls and bears reevaluate as before but this time, perceptions of value change and the group that was more aggressive before the pattern becomes the less aggressive group going out. How can one tell a reversal pattern from a continuation pattern as they are forming? The shape and position within the trend can yield more clues. However, the bottom line is to wait for the market to indicate by breaking out higher or lower.

This is covered in detail in Chapter 9.

Moving averages

A moving average is the average price of a stock or market over a defined period. In the stock market, a 200-day moving average is used to determine long-term trends. It smoothes out the short-term wiggles to help make the trend more clear. Short averages are used to measure or smooth shorter-term trends.

The term 'moving' comes from the calculation of the average. For a daily average, each day's value is calculated from a moving window of days going back in time. Each successive day's average is calculated from a successive range of daily data.

This is covered in more detail in Chapter 7.

Momentum

Momentum in markets is similar to momentum in physics. Markets in motion tend to stay in motion and markets at rest tend to stay at rest unless acted upon by an outside force. Price momentum indicators measure the speed and force of the trend.

For a quick explanation, consider a rubber ball tossed in the air. Its rate of ascent decreases even as it continues to rise. Market momentum readings can also fall as prices continue higher but sooner or later, the market, like the rubber ball, runs out of power and starts to come back down.

Indicators deserve their own chapters but it is really not critical to learn detail at this point in your career. You will see charts of the relative strength index (RSI) or Stochastics later in this book but like the automobile metaphor, you want to turn the key to start the car, not learn how the ignition mechanism works.

Two terms that are usually associated with momentum are *overbought* and *oversold*. They are strange terms, indeed, as they suggest that too much stock has been bought or sold. What they really mean is that the market has moved too far, too fast. Bullish or bearish activities of the minority have got out of line with bullish and bearish perceptions of the majority, so the trend cannot be sustained. Like a rubber band that has been stretched too tight, the market snaps back until activity and perceptions are in synch.

Divergence

Divergence on a chart exists when the relative trends of prices and of indicators are moving in different directions. It can be bullish or bearish, depending on the relative directions of the price and studies. Momentum and volume studies are analyzed extensively for divergence and this will be covered in Chapter 12.

part

2

The core of chart analysis

5

What are supply and demand in the markets?

In any capitalist marketplace, supply and demand rule. Consider a government study into the benefits of a certain wonder product that reports that it is 100 per cent safe and effective. High-profile celebrities provide endorsements to the product and there are no competitive products. Does this mean the maker of this product will see its profits rise?

> If the price of a stock or commodity is too high, there will be no demand and no buyers.

The answer is maybe. Profits will rise if, and only if, sales are made. If there is no demand for the product at the price at which it is offered, there will be no sales. The same reasoning holds true in the financial and commodity markets. If the price of a stock or commodity is too high, there will be no demand and no buyers. If the price is too low, there will be too much demand relative to supply and hence too many buyers.

In the example above, the maker of the wonder product may have a great product that will make lots of profits but a company is not its stock. They are related, of course, but they are not the same entity. Demand for the stock is not demand for the product that it makes. Only an imbalance in buyers over sellers makes the price rise.

What causes support and resistance levels to be penetrated?

If support and resistance levels are based on prices where bulls and bears buy and sell, respectively, with equal aggressiveness, something has to occur to change at least one side's opinion. In the stockmarket there are a few things that can change – the company, the market or the environment for stocks.

News of any of these changes does not itself move prices. Rather, it is the perception by the bulls and bears of the meaning of that news that moves prices.

The company

Company news can be a new product, a lawsuit, executive changes, financial problems, new stock offering and many others. Is the news good or bad? Is it fresh news or old news? That depends on whom you ask.

One example would be the effect on a company when its technology becomes obsolete. Equipment makers for vinyl LP records could not have fared well when the compact disc (CD) was introduced to the music industry. Dial-up database companies suffered when the Internet took hold.

The market

A rising tide in the market raises most boats. If the company 'boat' is not full of leaks, it will rise with the market during a bull phase. Likewise, unless it is of exceptional quality and value, it will fall with the market in a bear phase.

The environment for stocks

Since stocks are in different industries and business sectors, some benefit from certain interest rate changes while others are adversely affected. Some enjoy rising oil prices while others see their costs soar. In short, different stocks are strong during different parts of the business cycle.

A breakout in the price of gold will cause bullish conditions in gold mining stocks. A crash in the bond market will push up interest rates and hurt companies in need of new financing. New government regulations could limit profits or increase liability exposure of some companies and cause bearish conditions to form on their charts.

Summary

The question is 'why doesn't the market jump immediately from one equilibrium level to the next?' The answer is that information flow is not perfect and people do not all reach the same conclusions at the same time. As the masses slowly join a trend or breakout, the momentum builds until the price reaches levels that exhaust excess supply or excess demand. These are then called support and resistance.

Perceptions are reality

When a market trades between support and resistance, buyers and sellers are adjusting their actions according to what each perceives as being fair market value. At support, demand has increased to a point where it balances out supply. Conversely, at resistance, demand has decreased (relative to supply) to a point where it again balances out supply. These balance points are different at each price level.

As with rumours and advertising, the more times we hear something, the more we accept it. In the markets, the more times a market touches a support or resistance level, the more importantly that level will be perceived. Buyers and sellers become accustomed to acting in a certain way at each level. Unless something happens that causes perceived value to change, support and resistance levels will contain the market.

Consider an example in the stock market. Resistance for the stock of XYZ Company is at 50. The market bounces around below 50 for several weeks until it finally pushes above that price. Whether these new buyers acted on earnings news, an inflation report or a signal from a trading system does not matter. The charts show a breakout above resistance indicating a higher perception of value.

Something interesting often happens. If the market trades back down to 50, then buyers who missed the earlier breakout will see their second chance to get in. The market bounces up off the 50 level, which has now become support. Why is it now support? The reason is that the general level of valuation perception in the market has changed. What was once considered too high is now considered too low, based on the new levels of supply and demand.

Now presume that supply and demand balance out again at 55. Every time the market moves up to 55, sellers who missed their chance to unload their stock at that price earlier will become active. They fear that they will never see that price after the next pullback. Again, at 50, the greedy see that they can pick up some more cheap stock before it goes up again.

The chart of MATIF French bonds (Figure 5.1) is a good illustration. The two highlighted areas show how the market traded lower from a resistance level. Later, it failed to break through on its second attempt as sellers who missed the first opportunity took advantage of the second.

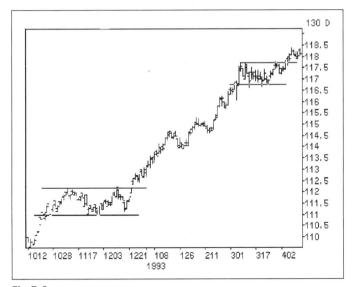

Fig 5.1 ■ MATIF French bonds

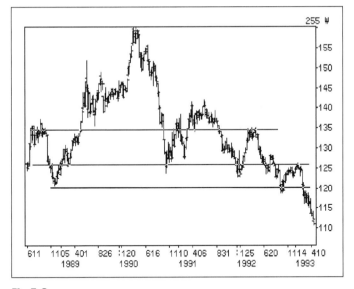

Fig 5.2 ■ Spot dollar/yen rate

Support and resistance levels can be found in all time frames, from tick to daily to monthly and longer. The 120, 126 and 135 levels in the spot dollar/yen rate (Figure 5.2) have been significant levels for the five years ending in 1993. When analyzing the major trends in a market, going back far enough in time will reveal prices in the past that have been significant market turning points.

The German DAX Index rallied several times after its July 1992 sharp decline and each time it was stopped at a level that provided support back in 1991 (Figure 5.3).

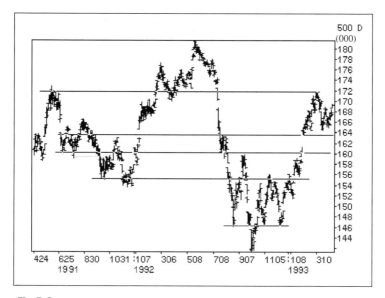

Fig 5.3 ■ German DAX Index

Support and resistance levels are ingrained in the market's memory but the more recent they are, the more impact they have in the current market. Be careful not to put too much weight in short-term tops and bottoms that happened long ago. Again, it has got to make sense and not just be a magic level because it was in the past.

The trend is your friend and so are trendlines

The old adage says, 'the trend is your friend.' Why? It is because trends tend to perpetuate unless something causes them to do otherwise. If you can identify a trend in its early stages, you can ride that trend for significant profits. Trendlines mark the trend on the chart so it can be followed easily once it is identified.

Trendlines

It has been shown that support and resistance lines are horizontal levels where prices stop falling and rising, respectively. Trendlines are simply support and resistance lines on an angle. In a trading range, the market naturally rises and falls within that price range. When it reaches the range bottom, the price is low enough to discourage the bears from being more aggressive. Likewise, the price is low enough for the bulls to become more aggressive. If the bulls are more aggressive than the bears, the market will then rise off this supporting level.

In a rallying market, the natural highs and lows occur at increasingly higher levels. A rising support line can be drawn through two or more of these increasing lows to become the supporting trendline for the rally. Each time the prices fall to the trendline, the bears become less aggressive and the bulls become more aggressive.

Consider this in terms of fear and greed. Each time the market dips, the buyers that failed to buy earlier at lower prices get their second chance to buy. Since they are afraid to miss the opportunity, they buy earlier and the price does not drop to the previous low. The market rises past the old high because sellers think they can get a higher price if they wait.

The general rule

In Figure 6.1, the peak in Canadian dollar futures was set in late 1991 and the top of the bar for that week serves as the starting point for the trendline. As the market trades lower, some market participants will eventually decide that it has become undervalued (cheap). They begin to buy, causing the market to trade a little higher (retracement). This counter-trend rally eventually loses, since the general perception of value is still falling. The bears once again take control and the market resumes its decline. Those recent buyers also reverse their positions, seeing that they were wrong, and add to the selling pressure.

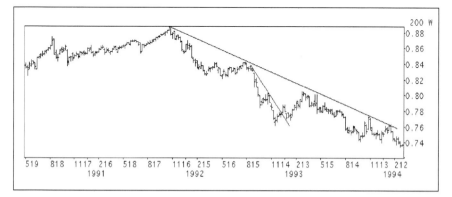

Fig 6.1 ■ Canadian dollar futures

This sort of trading action is exactly what happens at a resistance level. Since a declining trendline provides resistance, it should then be drawn from the recent high, which was set in late 1991 in Figure 6.1, to the high of the retracement rally where the buyers decided that they were wrong, which was in early August 1992. The trendline is extended lower as time goes on. As can be seen in the chart, this trendline has resisted all counter-trend rallies. That means that it describes where the bears took back control as the more aggressive traders.

Once a trend is established, you should trade with it, not against it.

Just as with support and resistance levels, the more times the market touches them, the stronger they become. Further, the stronger the trendline, the more significant the signal when the market penetrates it.

Once a trend is established, you should trade with it, not against it. For example, in Figure 6.1, the trend is falling. Selling when the market touches the trendline is a low-risk strategy. Buying the dips is a high-risk strategy since you would be fighting the market. Leave that to the professional traders.

To repeat: Once a trend is established, trade with it, not against it.

Log scales

When analyzing a stock or market over the long term, it is common to compare trends and price patterns at different price levels. If prices have not moved much in relation to their absolute price level, ordinary linear scaling is sufficient where each vertical distance on the chart represents the same price change. For example, Eurodollar futures traded in a seven-point range centered on a price of 93 for the 10-year period ending in 1994. In percentage terms, 7/93 = 7.5 per cent; a very small percentage of the average price.

When prices move in large percentages, trendline construction can be subjective and analysis unreliable. Logarithmic (log) scaling overcomes this problem. Rather than simply plotting price on the vertical axis in a linear fashion, prices are plotted to indicate percentage changes. This means that the vertical distance drawn for an item that doubles in price is the same whether it goes from 5 to 10 or from 100 to 200. A linear scale would plot the same vertical distance from 5 to 10 as it would for 100 to 105.

In Figures 6.2 and 6.3, the charts show the stock price for Microsoft beginning in mid-1986. Notice the price scales of Figures 6.2 and 6.3 are very different. Both start near 1 ½ (split adjusted) in 1986 and end near 54 in 1994. However, when prices rose from 2 to 4 in 1987, the linear scale on the left shows a very small move. The log scale on the right shows a very large move.

Fig 6.2 ■ Microsoft linear scale

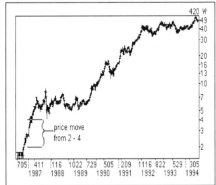

Fig 6.3 ■ Microsoft log scale

The vertical distance on the log scale for the move from 2 to 4 is the same as that of the move from 20 to 40. This simply means that prices doubled and provides for valid comparisons at any price level. It also allows for better trendline and pattern analysis. Note that the congestion zone taking place in 1988 and 1989 shows up much more clearly as a triangle pattern on the log scale. Note also that what appears to be a period of high volatility in 1992 and 1993 on the linear scale is put into better perspective on the log scale. Prices were no more volatile there than they were throughout the entire nine-year period shown.

Finding the trend

Figures 6.4 and 6.5 show five years of weekly data for the Hang Seng Index in Hong Kong. Figure 6.4 has a linear scale and Figure 6.5 has a log scale. When a trendline is drawn on the linear chart from the start of the long rally, prices traded higher away from the trend. This acceleration of the rally would incorrectly indicate that the market was moving too far, too fast and that a correction would occur soon. In early 1992, after being subjected to this excessive aggressiveness on the part of the bulls for more than a year, prices accelerated their rise even more. In 1993, prices again accelerated away from the new, steeper trendline, and still continued to rise. Any nervous investor reacting to this ever-increasing rate of price movement by selling would have sustained significant losses.

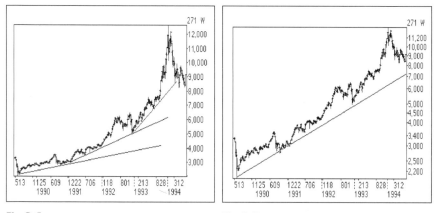

Fig 6.4 ■ Hang Seng linear   **Fig 6.5** ■ Hang Seng log

An investor using the log scaled chart in Figure 6.5 would have been able to see that the long-term trend in prices was consistent and this would have allowed a better analysis on the market. While the very strong decline in 1994 looked like it was accompanied by extreme volatility, it was actually less disastrous than the decline of early 1990, shown at the far left of the chart, when the market lost an even higher percentage of its value. A linear chart does not show this condition.

Conclusion

Logarithmic scaling is sometimes called ratio scaling and perhaps that is a better name. It tries to measure changes in value, rather than absolute prices. For example, a portfolio of 2 million euros is equally invested in one security purchased at 10 and another purchased at 100. Both markets rise 90 points so the first security is worth 100 and the second is worth 190. However, the first has gone up 10 times in value to 10 million and the second only 0.9 times to 1.9 million. In other words, significantly more profits were generated with the first security and the charts should reflect that fact. Log scaling allows the analyst to see a clearer picture of percentage changes than arithmetic scaling when markets move to different price levels.

Fan lines

There are many times when technicians are frustrated in their attempts to place trend lines. The market seems to define a trend then quickly breaks it to establish a shallower trend. This can happen several times before the market finally makes a clear reversal and leaves a slowly rolling-over chart pattern behind.

What's in a name?

The name for this pattern, fan lines, is derived from the appearance of the chart when the multiple trendlines are drawn from the same origin. It could easily have been called 'rollover lines' or 'trend reduction lines' with the latter indicating that the initial steep trend is flattening into a more sustainable level.

This can often be seen just after a breakout, as the euphoria and activity surge give way to a more sustainable trend. The same concept can be applied to the end of the trend with fan lines. At these junctures, the euphoria is gone and market sentiment swings slowly in the other direction.

US bonds were trending higher for most of 1995 (Figure 6.6). A steep trendline was broken in June but the market traded higher on a shallower trendline to meet the first line later that same month. Since supporting trendlines often act as resistance after they have been broken, the market fell again. This pattern was repeated in July until finally, prices fell below the third trendline.

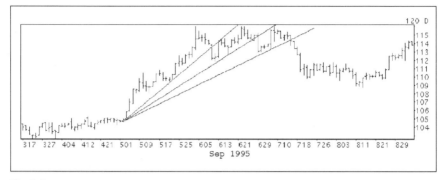

Fig 6.6 ■ US bonds

That the market reversed after the third trendline, illustrates the significance of the number three in technical analysis. With fan lines, traders who missed the first buy/sell opportunity (the trend break) get a second and finally a third chance as the market moves back up to the previous trendlines. Fan line patterns are, by definition, congestion zones as buyers and sellers position themselves. Can you see a triangle pattern in Figure 6.6 as the fan lines form?

When it fails

The real test of fan lines as a reversal pattern comes when the third trendline is touched. If that line successfully supports or resists prices, then the original trend is still intact. The S&P 500 showed such a pattern near the start of the 1984 rally (Figure 6.7). A classic fan shape was developing but the third trendline held. That line went on to support the rally for the next 12 months.

Trades must not be made until the pattern has been resolved.

The bottom line is that like any technical pattern, trades must not be made until the pattern has been resolved. Fan lines give ample warning of a possible reversal, plus a clear signal when it is time to trade.

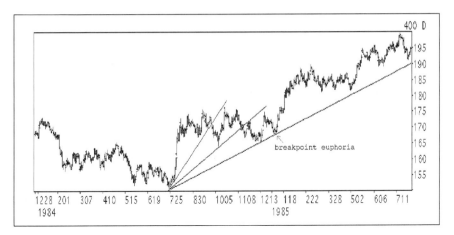

Fig 6.7 ■ **S&P 500**

See the forest and the trees

There are so many tools available to the technician that it is easy to overdo it. Vast quantities of data may be unnecessary to discern simple patterns. The 'noise' associated with daily data can confuse long-term analysis and too many indicators can obscure the trend they are attempting to measure. Keeping it simple allows the market's condition to jump right at you. Too much analysis may assign meaning where there is none.

> **Too much analysis may assign meaning where there is none.**

Less is more

Sometimes the data presented on a chart can get in the way of the analysis. The wiggles seen even on long-term charts obscure the trends the analyst is trying to find so a way is needed to cut through the clutter. Computerized filtered rocket science formulas can help, but only if you understand how to apply them. Rather, use the tools at hand to simplify the process to 'see the forest' while 'navigating through the trees'.

Line charts

A large percentage of technicians use daily bar charts. They use open, high, low and close data to summarize what happened during the trading day. Intraday movements can be knee-jerk reactions to news or market conditions rather than illustrative of the actual trend or technical pattern in force at the time. Using only closing data reduces the resolution of the chart but it also reduces the visual clutter. This makes trends and patterns easier to spot.

Figures 7.1 and 7.2 show the NASDAQ Composite index from April 1995 to December 1996 in both bar and line formats. Note that the line chart is drawn with a continuous line to make trends even easier to spot. On the bar chart, the corrective pattern from August 1995 to January 1996 is a triangle. On the line chart, the pattern is a rectangle. For comparison, the bottom of the bar chart's pattern is drawn on the line chart. The difference is clear.

More important than the shapes of the patterns are the depths of the two retracements. Forecasting potential price moves, the depth (height) of the chart pattern is often used to measure first and second targets after a breakout. This is because people tend to think in terms of ranges and carry that thinking forward to the next price level.

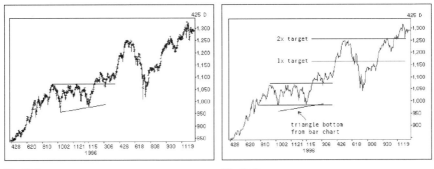

Fig 7.1 ■ NASDAQ bar format   **Fig 7.2** ■ NASDAQ line format

Of course, this is all hindsight. Would one have known to use a line chart for forecasting at the time? The answer is in the price action of 10 October, 1995; the date of the big intraday spike down. When the market moves in such big swings, the likely cause is a panic-led overshoot of a technical target. A line chart ignores this condition and should have been employed immediately. It focuses on the finally accepted value after all news and activity is digested.

Multiple time frames

Technicians need to keep their perspective. By focusing only on charts matching their investment horizon, they may fail to spot changes in the major trend. For example, using daily bar charts with nine months of data could show a strong rally while the same chart over a two-year period may show a large trading range. Wouldn't it be good to know if the current rally is occurring at the bottom of the range, bumping up against the top of the range or even breaking through the range completely? It certainly would help in knowing if your short-term investing is in line with the long-term trend.

Pull back from your analysis periodically to perform a sanity check. Does your strategy make sense in the larger scheme of things? If not, you will need to watch your investments like a trader and be prepared to switch gears in a hurry.

Moving averages

Although stock and commodity prices follow trends higher and lower, they can be quite volatile. For example, the long-term trend in stocks for the last decade has been up but medium- and short-term trends, such as the extreme events of October 1987, can move in exactly the opposite direction. To smooth out this volatility, the moving average is used. Often, it can take the place of trendlines.

Simple moving averages

There are several types of moving averages currently in use. The most basic is the simple moving average which takes the prices from the previous user-defined number of periods, sums them up and divides by the number of periods. A 10-day average is simply the average closing price for the past 10 days. Each successive day is calculated fresh from the 10 most recent days. This is how the average 'moves'. The number of periods to use in the average depends on the stock or commodity being analyzed. Typically, it is related to the cycle of the underlying item, such as a four-year stock market cycle, seasonal heating oil cycle and an agricultural harvest cycle.

The average is overlaid on the price chart and crossovers between the average and the underlying price are observed. When prices are rising they are usually above the average. This is to be expected since the average includes data from the previous, lower-priced days. As long as prices remain above the average, there is strength in the market. Buyers are willing to pay more for the stock or commodity as the market continues to value it higher.

When prices cross below the average, it means that the market no longer expects prices to continue higher, at least temporarily. The more market participants taking this new view, the higher the volume will be and the better the signal. Remember, the valuation in the market is based on what market participants think will happen in the future. If the price is expected to rise, buyers will buy it now at the lower price which in turn causes demand to rise. Rising demand means higher prices and the rally will been sustained.

Figure 7.3 is a 200-day line chart of Merrill Lynch. The 21-day average being used is typical for a large US stock and provided support for the mid-1993 rally. Since an average smoothes out volatility, it serves as a proxy for the trend itself, so when prices crossed below the average in early October, a warning was given that the stock would reverse. When the average itself turned lower in mid-October, the signal was confirmed. Note that prices crossed the average several times without the stock reversing. None of these false signals were confirmed by other indicators such as the Relative Strength Index (RSI) or volume.

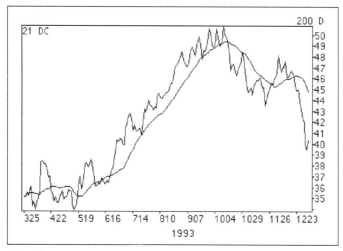

Fig 7.3 ■ Merrill Lynch

Weighted and exponential averages

This topic is included in the chapter to introduce you to a commonly used technical tool.

Moving averages are lagging indicators. They summarize previous data and plot it on current prices so an analyst using only moving averages will probably not be able to call tops and bottoms in the markets. The change in the trend will be seen only after it has happened. The potential profit lost by the inability to pick tops and bottoms is offset by the reduction in volatility seen and the reduced risk of making a bad trade.

In order to reduce the lag of the simple average, more weight can be assigned to recent data and less to older data. A weighted 10-day moving average assigns a weight of 1 to the first day, 2 to the second and so forth until the most current day which is assigned a weight of 10. The 10 weighted values are added together and the sum is divided by the sum of the weights, which in this case is 55.

Exponential averages are similar to weighted averages in that they give more importance to recent data. The difference is in how it assigns the weights. It is not important here to go into details of the formula except to say that a weighted average is an arithmetic weighting, and exponential average is a geometric weighting. This really only means that it reacts even faster to price changes than the other averages.

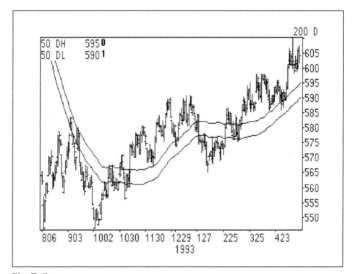

Fig 7.4 ■ CBT **soybeans**

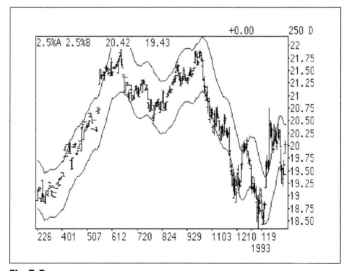

Fig 7.5 ■ **Nymex crude oil**

Moving-average envelopes

Some markets react differently in bull and bear markets. For these, it is useful to base moving averages on high and low prices instead of closing prices. For example, to confirm a new bull market the analyst might require prices to cross above the moving average of the highs. This adds additional filtering of volatility without having to use longer, and less sensitive, averages.

This leads us to moving-average envelopes which are simply a pair of moving averages above and below price (sometimes envelopes are referred to as trading bands). Figure 7.4 shows May 1993 CBT soybeans with 50-day high and 50-day low simple averages. Breakouts higher are indicated by prices crossing above the high average. Conversely, crosses below the bottom low average indicate new market declines. Note how crossovers below the top average in March 1993 were not confirmed by crosses below the bottom average. This envelope did not signal 'sell', therefore keeping the investor in the market for the next rally.

Another way to create envelopes is to take a moving average of the close and then add and subtract a certain percentage of the average value. Figure 7.5 shows March 1993 NYMEX crude oil for one year. The envelope shown is a 2½ per cent band centered on a 14-day moving average. The moving average selected served as a good proxy for the short-term trends for crude oil that year and the 2½ per cent value is a commonly used parameter across markets. By selecting the envelope parameters to contain the normal volatility of the market, the analyst can determine if overbought or oversold conditions are reached when prices move out of the envelope's borders. The analysis can be made more sensitive by decreasing the envelope width and less sensitive by increasing it.

Again, anything more than understanding simple moving averages is more than you will need to know at this point. Advanced averages and bands are presented here to give you a taste for how others adapt and apply them so you will have a framework for your own advanced education.

8 Chart patterns – when the market needs a rest

Markets go up and markets go down but they also go sideways. Both bulls and bears can lose their desires to buy and sell aggressively as value is established. They wait for the next clues the market will leave as it decides where it wants to go next. This chapter contains key information describing how to read those clues on a chart.

Just like a car heading out for a long journey, trending markets need to rest occasionally to refuel. These 'rest stops' are called congestion zones. Congestion zones are price levels where the bulls and the bears are taking their profits, licking their wounds and rethinking their strategies.

Most technical patterns form when the market trades in the same price range over several time periods (minutes, hours, days, etc.). The bars temporarily stop trending in either direction and tend to bunch up in a small region. This is called congestion. The shape of the congestion zone gives the technician clues on where the market will head next, either in the same or in the opposite direction. Once the shape has been determined, the technician waits for confirmation in the form of a breakout from the zone (prices leave the congestion zone) and possibly from a technical study such as the relative strength index (RSI).

Trending markets need to rest occasionally to refuel.

Technicians call a portion of them continuation patterns because the odds favour a continuation of the existing trend when these patterns are finished. These are patterns you can see quickly without using any special measuring devices.

Rectangles

A rectangle pattern is simply a region bounded by a support line on the bottom and a resistance line on the top. The market trades up and down between these two levels for a number of periods, depending on the type of chart being used. Rectangles are also called trading ranges and the lessons of support and resistance aptly describe what is happening within.

Figure 8.1 shows the December MATIF Bond contract, tick by tick, at the end of September 1993. The market began its short-term rally on the 24th of the month and on the 27th it began consolidating those gains in a rectangle pattern. After bouncing around all day in a less than 20-tick range, it broke out to the upside the next day with a strong morning rally.

This rectangle pattern can be seen in longer charts too. Figure 8.2 shows a weekly chart of the US dollar index from early 1989 to late 1991. Here, the market was falling from mid-1989 until it entered a rectangle pattern. Note that the last rally attempt within the rectangle failed to reach the top boundary. This is a sign of weakness in the market and is a very good indication that the trend will continue lower.

It is important to let the market prove that the rectangle is a continuation pattern by letting it actually break out. Rectangles and the other patterns described below usually break in the direction of the original trend but not all of the time.

Note this: usually, but not all the time.

Triangles

This type of continuation pattern has converging lines of support and resistance. Some traders refer to triangles as 'coils' because the trading action gets tighter and tighter until the market breaks out with great force. What is happening is that both the bulls and the bears are becoming more and more unsure about the market. They buy and sell sooner, so the market moves in smaller wiggles. Uncertainty builds and tensions increase as all participants wait for the next clues of market direction. When the market finally breaks free from the coil, pent-up supply or demand is released and the market springs lower or higher, respectively.

Again, the breakout usually, but not always, occurs in the direction of the original trend. The triangle highlighted in the US dollar index had a very strong breakout lower (Figure 8.2).

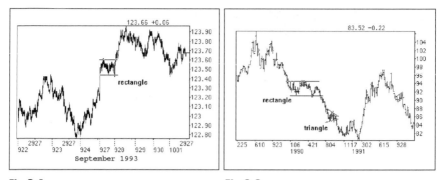

Fig 8.1 ■ Matif Paris bond

Fig 8.2 ■ US dollar index

Triangles come in several varieties. The US dollar chart showed a symmetrical shape. The December CBT US Treasury bond was in an ascending triangle pattern during much of the first half of 1993 (Figure 8.3 – daily data). An ascending triangle has a relatively flat top boundary with a rising bottom boundary. Conversely, a descending triangle (see Figure 8.4) has a relatively flat bottom boundary and a falling top boundary. Both of these point in the direction of the likely breakout.

Another important point to keep in mind when analyzing triangles is that a breakout is significant if it occurs approximately two-thirds of the way from the left side of the triangle to the apex (the apex is where the two lines would meet if they were extended). If the price action continues to bounce around in the triangle close to the apex, a breakout is less significant and other technical indicators should be used.

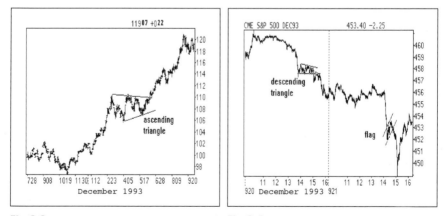

Fig 8.3 ■ CBT Treasury bond

Fig 8.4 ■ CME S&P 500

Flags

The most common of the continuation patterns is called a flag because it resembles a flag flying on a flagpole. When a market is trending higher, it is more common for it to slowly give back some of those gains as the bulls take some profits. Since traders do not all do this at the same time, the market displays a small counter trend move lower as more of them take their profits. When this is over, the market generally breaks out in the direction of the original trend as the bulls re-take their long positions and new bulls enter the market at the new attractive price level.

The CME December S&P 500 fell sharply on 21 September due to the news of political unrest in Russia (Figure 8.4 tick by tick). Even during this fast market trading, prices staged a rebound as some of the bears took their profits and some bulls came in to buy at the lower price, thinking that the market had gone down enough. Prices eventually broke out lower from the flag and the market continued to plummet.

For those of you who remember what an intraday chart of the 1987 stock market crash looked like (The Dow Jones Industrial Average), this same pattern emerged mid-day as even that raging bear needed to rest for a while.

Cup with handle

Often, a single technical formation incorporates the rules of other patterns. This illustrates the concept that no single technical signal is good enough to stand by itself. Rather, when several indicators signal concurrently, each is reinforced and the likelihood of a correct trading decision is increased geometrically. One such pattern is called the 'cup with handle'.

The cup with handle pattern is commonly applied to the stock market although any market with daily volume data should theoretically work the same. The pattern gets its name from its appearance of a coffee cup with a handle on the right.

Basing pattern

After a rally, the stock settles into a downward correction pattern that usually lasts three to six months. This forms the left side and bottom of the cup. When prices start to rise again, volume increases until the old high is reached. This forms the right side of the cup.

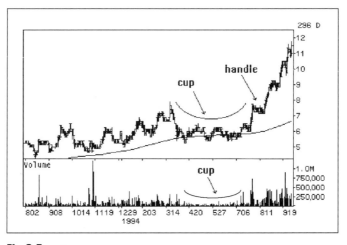

Fig 8.5 ■ FSI International

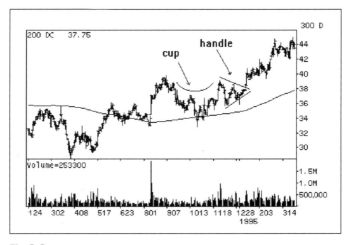

Fig 8.6 ■ Household International

What has happened so far is that the market rallied and then corrected on lower volume. Low volume indicates that the bears have not really got aggressive and therefore do not perceive the market as being above fair value.

Figure 8.5 shows a clear pattern in FSI International. The bottom of the cup shows unusually low volume, which refutes the notion that the trend had reversed lower. In this case, the right side of the cup starts when prices break out of the trading range at the cup's bottom. Volume spikes up, which is exactly the confirmation needed for any trendline or pattern break.

At the old highs, selling pressure increases from both those who failed to sell at the old high (second chance to sell) and those who bought at the cup bottom (profit takers). Now the market drifts lower in a smaller correction called the handle. Remember, the market has been rallying on increasing volume since the cup bottom. The handle is a normal correction. When the handle pattern is broken, volume spikes again and the stock is off and running.

Handles should never dip too far into the cup and usually last a few short weeks. Deep handles indicate a larger trading range rather than a small correction in a rising market.

In the real world, the cup with handle is not always an exact pattern. Household International (Figure 8.6) had two deviations from the ideal. First, the right side of the cup did not quite reach the old high. Second, the handle was shaped like a triangle rather than a flag. As a metaphor, the latter would be easier to hold, but both show downward movement of prices on lower volumes. As long as the other criteria are met, these imperfections can be tolerated.

The buy signal in Figure 8.5 was given when the stock made a new high after the handle breakout. In Figure 8.6, the signal was given when prices broke the downtrend line formed by the cup's two peaks.

Rules of the game

Besides those mentioned above, there are several other rules to apply to the pattern. First, the shape and depth of the cup are important. The depth of the cup should be in proportion to the width. Again, technical analysis embraces relative changes in the market so be sure your assumptions make sense. There may be specific levels that many market experts use but general levels suffice here. The depth of the cup should be 20–30 per cent of the peak price because shallower cups do not give the weak bulls enough incentive to get out. Deeper cups can require the stock to double in price before the buy signal is even completed.

> The shape and depth of the cup are important.

Cups should not be too sharp either. The 'v-shaped' bottom does not give the stock sufficient time to form a solid base. The bottom line is that the cup should look like a cup, not a dish or a champagne glass.

The final indicator to watch is the 200-day moving average. (It is not important to dwell on why 200-days is chosen over 253 (trading days per year) or 180 (nine trading months). This moving average is the most popular barometer for the stock market and that is sufficient.)

As in other analyses, when a stock gets too far above the average, a correction usually follows. A valid handle breakout occurs at prices less than 65 per cent above the average. Momentum indicators such as rate of change and relative strength index are likely to show overbought conditions at higher percentages.

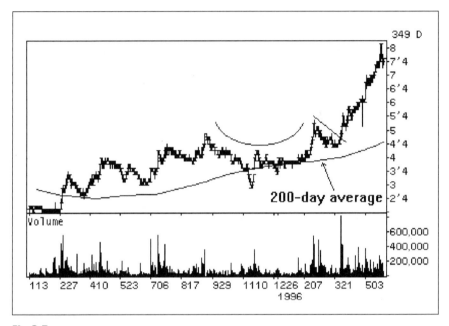

Fig 8.7 ■ Genesco

Figure 8.7 shows Genesco Inc. The cup's bottom found support on the 200-day average (except for the early November selling climax). Even though the right side overshot the left, volume spiked during both the rise and at the handle breakout.

The cup with handle pattern is a clear continuation pattern. Should the handle dip below the 200-day average, chances are that the average is flat and the market is not in a true intermediate term rally. In that case, any continuation pattern breakout would be suspect.

As a basing pattern, the cup with handle is well defined by the multiple technical indicators that comprise it. This allows its signals to be quite clear.

Chart patterns – when the market is changing its mind

'A correction is when you are losing money. A bear market is when I am losing money.' – William Noble, Research Director, Logical Information Machines

If some chart patterns are merely a rest stop for the market, others are turning points. If you already own a position in the market and one of these patterns form, it is probably time to consider selling. Remember, this is the time to prepare, not to execute. Chart patterns must be allowed to break before you act. True, you will not buy the low nor sell the high but those points in the market are for the professional who is very closely tied to the action.

In this chapter we will learn to recognize patterns that usually form at the end of trends. Technicians call them reversal patterns.

Head and shoulders

One of the most widely recognized reversal patterns is the 'head and shoulders.' It is named for its resemblance to a head with two shoulders on either side. Aside from appearances, this pattern demonstrates several technical factors such as failing momentum, support/resistance breaks and trend breaks.

In a rising market, prices make higher highs and higher lows as the trend continues up (Figure 9.1). The left shoulder is simply part of this pattern. Prices rise to the top of the shoulder and fall in a normal retracement (correction).

Next, prices rise to another new high (Figure 9.2). It cannot be predicted yet that this is going to be the 'head' of the pattern and the final push in the rally. There will be an indication that something is not quite right with the rally because momentum or volume readings will most likely be falling, setting up a divergence with the price. The bulls are losing power even though the market continued higher. As prices fall back, they now fail to set a higher low and fall back to the previous low. We call this the 'neckline'.

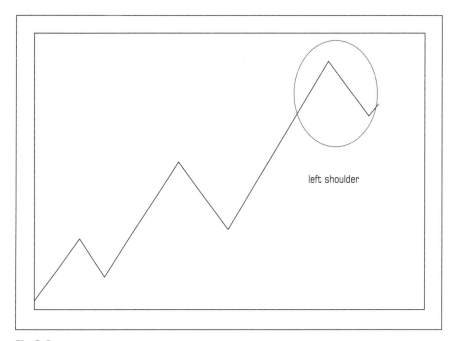

Fig 9.1 ■ Left shoulder

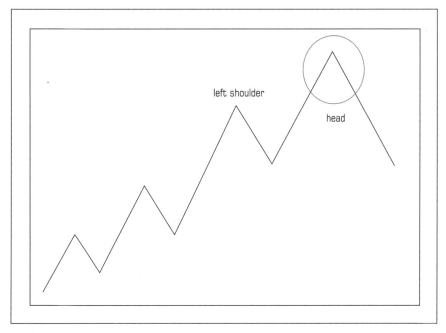

Fig 9.2 ■ Head

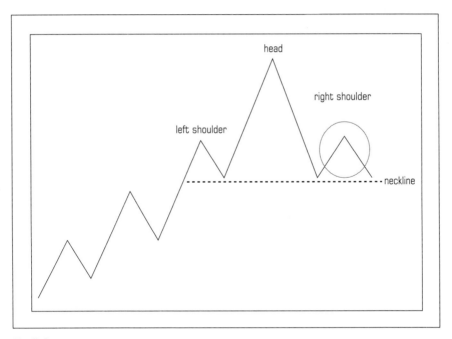

Fig 9.3 ■ Right shoulder

To summarise so far, momentum is falling, prices failed to make a higher low and the retracement after the head has most likely broken a trendline. At minimum, it has formally defined the neckline as a support line.

Now, as the market once again attempts to make a higher high, momentum decreases further. Prices fail to even reach the previous high (the head) and fall to the neck. The weaker the market, the smaller the right shoulder (Figure 9.3). When the neckline is broken to the down side, the pattern is completed and a reversal occurs. It is important to note that many technical indicators are used (momentum, volume, trendbreak, etc.) to reach this conclusion, not just a shape on the chart.

Step back from the chart for a moment. How many people do you know that have their necks at the bottom of their shoulders? Do you think Picasso was a technician?

The daily chart of the cash Australian dollar (Figure 9.4) shows an inverted head and shoulders in a falling market. Note that the momentum indicator (RSI) is rising. The right shoulder had broken the down trendline in mid-July and currently has broken above the neckline, completing the pattern.

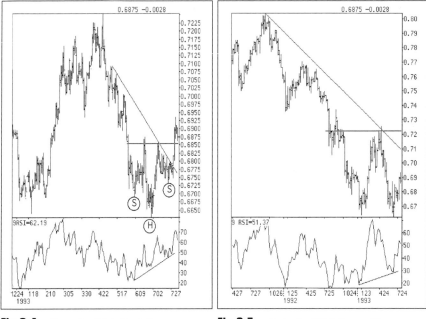

Fig 9.4 ■ Australian/US dollar daily   **Fig 9.5** ■ Australian/US dollar weekly

Double tops and bottoms

Another important reversal pattern is the 'M' or 'W' shaped pattern called a double top or double bottom, respectively. This is essentially a head and shoulders without the head. One important difference is that while a head and shoulders is more dramatic, it is also less strict in its definition. The neckline need not be horizontal but can be on an angle. The double top and bottom requires that it be based on a true support or resistance level.

The weekly chart of the Australian dollar (Figure 9.5) shows a double bottom that formed over an eight-month period. Prices corrected from their January lows to their April highs. Note that these highs met resistance at a previous congestion zone formed a year earlier (support becomes resistance). The June lows matched those from January and prices are currently rising. The technician would wait until the two-year-old down trendline is broken before buying. Other confirming indicators are an increasing RSI and the inverted head and shoulders bottom in the daily chart which formed the second bottom in the weekly chart.

This pattern requires patience because prices have two hurdles to overcome before a long-term trend can be established. First, the current down trend must be broken. If it is, this market is likely to rise to the previous highs of April. Next, it must break that resistance level. If it does not, the double bottom did not do its job. Remember, chart patterns by themselves can be misleading. They require confirmation.

One-day reversals

This pattern is made of only one bar but it is critically important that it be placed at the proper point on the chart. After a rally, the market makes a higher high but something happens during the day. All of a sudden, market sentiment shifts to the bears and the price ends up closing lower for a net loss on the day.

The converse is true at bottoms as the market makes a lower low but closes higher on the day. Both suggest that something has happened to change sentiment.

One-day reversals may sound like a short-term trading pattern but like most technical tools, they can be applied in many time frames. A one-month reversal would be an excellent tool for long-term investors.

Figure 9.6 shows a one-day reversal in Intel Corp. Note how the reversal bar itself made a higher high for the move.

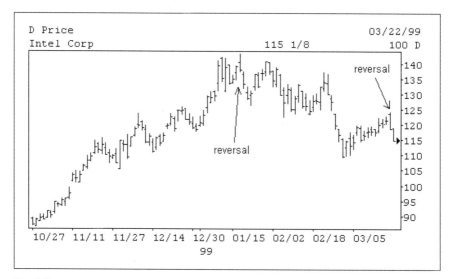

Fig 9.6 ■ One-day reversal in Intel Corp

Triangles and rectangles

Weren't triangles and rectangles in the last chapter on continuation patterns? If you caught that, thank you for paying attention. Triangles and rectangles are usually considered warnings of a continuation of the trend but nothing is guaranteed. Most of the time the market does break out in the direction of the previous trend, but not always. This section is here to drive home the point that you cannot buy or sell in anticipation of a breakout. You must wait for it to happen.

Figure 9.7 shows the US bond in a very clear triangle pattern. There was a small warning that the triangle would break lower, rather than continue higher, from the descending shape of the triangle itself. The upper border was declining, indicating that the bears were becoming more aggressive.

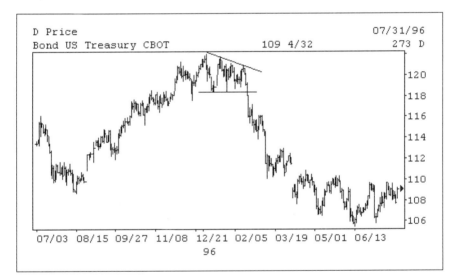

Fig 9.7 ■ US bond in triangle pattern

Rounded tops and bottoms

These are the patterns you see after they are over. Not very helpful, right? Well, you can actually see them before they are over if you know what to watch. They represent a slow, gradual shift in the market, perhaps even a loss of interest.

> In a rally, bulls just fade away without bears stepping in to take charge.

In a rally, bulls just fade away without bears stepping in to take charge. In a decline, it is just the opposite as bears stop selling aggressively without bulls stepping in to take over. The frustrating part is that trendlines are broken without the euphoria or increased activity associated with a clear reversal of trend. Fan lines appear to fail as well. When analysis becomes unclear, it is always a good idea to fall back on the basic definitions of trend. Look for the higher highs and higher lows at bottoms. Look for lower highs and lower lows at tops.

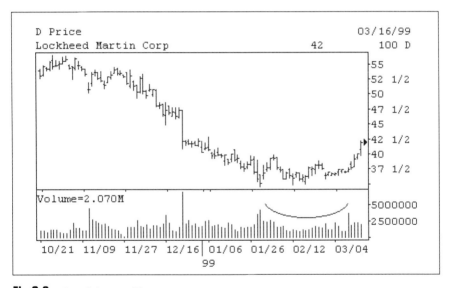

Fig 9.8 ■ Rounded tops and bottoms

Spikes

These are the opposite of the rounded reversals as they are very sharp. If the saucer is a pudgy 'U' shape, spikes are skinny 'V' shapes. Some rapid shift in sentiment triggered by news or intermarket changes smacks the market.

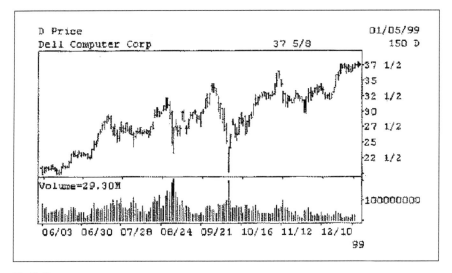

Fig 9.9 ■ Spikes

Spikes are also difficult to manage so you will need to analyze what was happening just before the spike itself. Was there a divergence in some of the indicators? Did the market's trend suddenly accelerate going into the spike (Figure 9.10) or was it fairly flat (Figure 9.11)? The former might indicate a panic in the market while the latter might indicate that the trend was accelerating, not reversing.

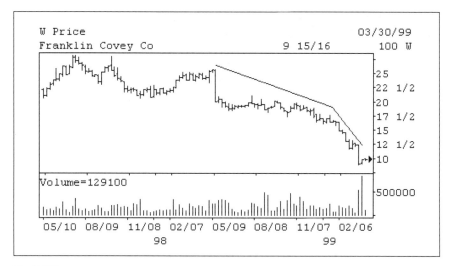

Fig 9.10 ■ Spike after accelerating market trend

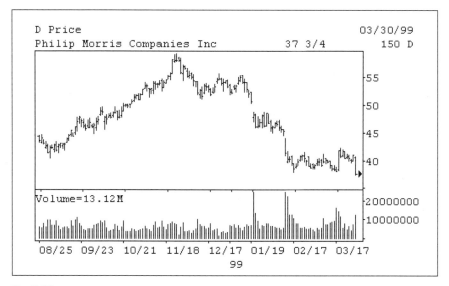

Fig 9.11 ■ Spike after flat market trend

10 Chart patterns – explosions

Sometimes, perceptions in the market change so rapidly that the market seems to explode higher or lower. The extreme form of this action is a market crash but this rapid shift of perception can be seen after takeover announcements or earnings news following unrealistic projections. Rather than a gradual spread of news and market information, it spreads rapidly. This is sometimes exaggerated by news emerging between trading sessions so there was no time for a gradual reaction. As the market opens, all of the pent-up buying or selling is released and the market rockets higher or lower, respectively.

Technicians call these situations gaps because they leave a void on the charts. A gap is simply a price level where a market does not trade. In a rising market, a gap occurs when prices open at a higher level than the previous day's high and do not trade lower to fill the space. The reverse is true for a falling market. Gaps signal market strength and weakness, respectively.

Breakaway gaps

Breakaway gaps (Figure 10.1) occur at the completion of an organized price pattern and usually signal the start of a significant price move. They are important because they emphasize that there was a breakout and this becomes an even stronger signal when it occurs with higher volume. Heavy volume breakaway gaps are usually important levels of support and resistance over the longer term as well.

Fig 10.1 ■ CSCE coffee

Fig 10.2 ■ COMEX gold

When market participants are adjusting their activities in a consolidation pattern such as a rectangle, triangle or head and shoulders, they buy and sell to lock in profits and limit losses within a defined price range. Whether these ranges are constant (rectangle) or tight-

> A gap signifies that a very large share of market participants have changed their opinions together.

ening (triangle), value in the market remains at accepted levels. At the breakout, market opinion has shifted. A gap signifies that a very large share of market participants have changed their opinions together and is a very powerful indicator.

Continuation gaps

Once a rally or decline is underway, the market pauses and retraces as participants again position themselves. These sorts of patterns are to expected, but sometimes market opinion is so strong that there is no time for normal profit taking and last chances to establish a position (long or short, depending on the market). When the majority of participants think that a market will continue its move, the market can simply jump to those new prices immediately and this is known as a continuation gap. Because these types of gaps typically occur at the halfway point of a move, they are sometimes called measuring gaps. Continuation gaps can occur alone, as a series of gaps or not at all.

Exhaustion gaps

The last of the classified types is called an exhaustion gap because it occurs near the end of the move to signal a last push toward new highs or lows. It is sometimes too difficult to identify this type of gap because it appears in a trending market just like a continuation gap. Price action in the days immediately following the gap helps the analyst determine which kind of gap it was. Whereas continuation gaps are following by a continuing strong trend, exhaustion gaps are followed by more congested, sideways market action. Such signals as one-day reversals help identify which gap has occurred.

Prices usually trade back to fill the gap and when they do, it is a good sign that the move is over. The gap represents the market 'frenzy' where all participants are buying or selling at any price just to be involved. The smart money uses this activity to take profits, leaving only the weak participants left to try to push the market further. (See Figure 10.2).

A common reversal pattern seen with exhaustion gaps is called an 'island reversal'. After a market gap (exhaustion), it usually trades for a few days in a small range. If the relative numbers of weak participants is high, those last-minute buyers or sellers quickly reverse their positions to cause a gap in the opposite direction. The shape of the gap, congestion and reverse gap looks like an island surrounded by water. This sort of pattern usually signals a strong change in trend.

Other gaps

The final category for gaps does not really have a name but has been called a 'common' or 'unclassified' gap. These types of gaps occur within price patterns or congestion zones and are the least meaningful of all gaps. They generally signify a lack of direction in the market or lack of conviction of the market participants. News and sentiment affect these markets more than others simply because they are less liquid at that time.

While this chapter has focused on daily charts, gap analysis is valid for all time frames such as five minute and hourly. As markets trade closer to 24 hours, gaps become less likely. Overnight news has less chance to affect them, so intraday analysis may become more prevalent.

Corrections in perspective

Most practitioners of technical analysis will agree that no market moves in one direction forever. After a rally or decline, the market will pause as winners take profits, losers cut their losses and the second round of positioning takes place. Terms like correction, consolidation and retracement are fairly interchangeable although some would argue that the shape of the pattern created distinguishes them. In most applications, a correction takes place after a significant change in accepted market value. The correction's shape and size are intimately related to the move being corrected.

No market moves in one direction forever.

The good technical analyst will look at different indicators in different time periods. However, we all become comfortable with certain time periods for certain indicators or securities.

The right way

Without going into precise measuring techniques and strict interpretations, a correction simply takes place after prices have moved. Figure 11.1 shows how a normal correction fits into the ebb and flow of the CSCE coffee market in 1997. In March, the market set an intermediate term peak and broke a rising trendline to the downside. This turned into a declining flag pattern that is typical in most markets. The bottom of the flag occurred at approximately the 50 per cent pullback level of the December 1996–March 1997 rally. This is a common correction amount. Both the subjectivity of the flag and imprecision of the 50 per cent pullback low are entirely normal in their deviations from textbook patterns. After the top of the flag was broken to the upside, the rally continued.

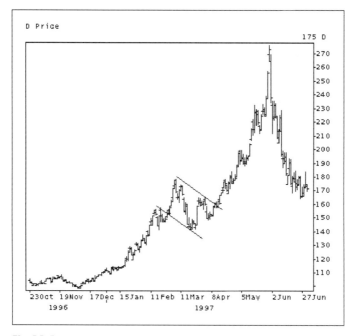

Fig 11.1 ■ CSCE coffee market

The point of all this is that a normal correction, whether it takes on a flag, triangle or rectangle shape, occurs after a reasonable move over a reasonable length of time. It retraces a reasonable portion of that move and then the market continues on for another reasonable rally. ('Reasonable' is not specifically intended to be defined here as this is not quantitative proof. Visual measurement and classification of the chart will be good enough.)

The wrong way

Problems arise when the technician gets impatient or tries to force meaning on the chart that the market has not put there. In Figure 11.2, the COMEX gold market was in a steady downtrend until it dropped sharply in early July 1997. The price action that followed appeared to be a rising flag, which would be an expected pattern at that point. On 15 July, the market broke below the flag in what looked like a continuation of the bear market. The problem with this analysis was that a six-day flag pattern that retraced about $9 was not sufficient to correct a decline that was three months old and $40 long (based on the last intermediate peak in May).

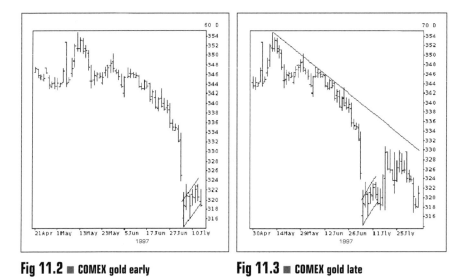

Fig 11.2 ■ COMEX gold early   **Fig 11.3** ■ COMEX gold late

Figure 11.3 shows the same chart a few weeks later. The flag pattern is still a valid interpretation but it grew to cover nearly one month and $15. The top of the flag reached approximately a one-third recovery (another common level seen on all markets). Additionally, it was close to the declining trendline that defined the market before the July plunge. Now we have a reasonable move, reasonable correction and the possibility of another reasonable move to the downside.

Keep in mind that the next leg down may not materialize. The point is that selling the apparent break 15 July was premature. While there are no guarantees, the break 5 August was a much higher confidence trade.

part

3

Technical analysis in the real world

What is there other than price?

Price action is only one part of market analysis. There are several dimensions that further enhance the price chart including volume, momentum, time and even how everyone feels about the market. Some of these are hard to quantify. Others are in the

Every indicator tells a story.

newspaper listings and free Internet web sites. When the market goes one way and the supporting indicator goes the other then something is happening beneath the surface and an early trading opportunity may be in the works.

Listen to them — every indicator tells a story. Consider, below, a few of the areas that affect your individual investments.

The big picture

The market. When your friend asks 'How was the market today?' and you are in the USA, your answer is something like 'The Dow was up 50.' In the UK, the FTSE (pronounced 'footsie') was up 50. In Japan, the Nikkei was up 50. Are they all talking about the same market? Well, no. Each is referring to a specific market index and each index is taking only a small slice of the stock market in its respective country.

The Dow Jones Industrial Average has only 30 stocks, yet is one of the most widely used methods to describe the 'market'. Staying with the US market, the Standard and Poor's 500 is broader in coverage but there are several thousand stocks listed on the major stock exchanges and many thousands more traded over the counter. Is the Wilshire 5000 Index closer to the market?

The answer is, 'it depends'. What is in your portfolio? If you only trade blue chip stocks then the Dow or the FTSE 100 or the Nikkei 225 are good enough. If you trade technology stocks, then maybe the NASDAQ composite or the Pacific Stock Exchange Hi Tech indices would be better.

Like magazines, there are market indices to suit every investment style. What is the market? The market is what you care about. If I own a small company mutual fund that is losing value while the blue chip indices are rising, is my market rising?

So how is the market defined? The answer is to follow several sectors. If the blue chips, the small caps, the food stocks and the utilities are all rising, then you can say that the market is rising. Once this is determined, then you can be comfortable employing bullish strategies across the board. As mentioned earlier, the rising tide raises most boats.

Does the market have bad breadth?

Although the stock market can be considered to be a living, breathing entity, the term 'breadth' refers to how all-embracing is the participation of all stocks in the market. The more stocks that rally, the broader the participation and the stronger the overall market becomes. One can measure how many stocks are rising and how many are falling. One can measure how much volume the rising stocks are getting, compared to the volume the declining stocks are getting, to see if each is getting their fair share. One can even measure how the blue chip names are doing compared to the small stocks or how different industry sectors are performing. If only a small slice of the overall market is rallying to send the major indices higher, the rally is not broad based and is therefore risky.

Unlike the government bond market or the cocoa market, the stock market is multi-dimensional. If you are trading treasury bonds, that is all there is. Sure, there are a few different maturities and coupon rates to worry about, but the overwhelming majority of trading activity centres on only one 'on the run' bond. For cocoa futures, yes, there are different futures months to trade but again, it is all cocoa.

The stock market is completely different. It has been said that it is not a 'stock market' but a 'market of stocks'. Not only do you need to know if the world is right for owning equities but you must consider which equities to buy. In cocoa, you buy cocoa. Perhaps you get to decide to buy cash cocoa or cocoa futures, but in the end, you own cocoa. With stocks, there is no agreement over what indicator actually describes the stock market, let alone can you buy an actual piece of the market.

Traders and investors alike have been searching for ways to describe 'the market' for decades. In the stock market, analysts use the 'top down' approach where they look at the market, then the industry group and, finally, the individual stock. In contrast, the phrase 'it's not a stock market but a market of stocks' takes a 'bottom up' approach based on the notion that the market is really the sum of the actions of all groups and stocks. To reconcile these two methods, tools are needed to generalize the behaviour of all stocks and they all fall into the category of market breadth indicators. One of the more commonly-used tools is called the advance-decline line.

The basics of market breadth

During bull markets, it is a rare, if not impossible, for all stocks to be rising. Speculators may have pushed up some issues to overbought conditions early and they are caught in short-term corrections. Some industries and their stocks flourish during one part of the business cycle while others languish. What the market needs in order to be classified as 'healthy' are the basic technical underpinnings of rising trends, rising volume and rising participation from the masses. For the stock market, this means both widespread interest from investors and traders and broad interest in the majority of issues available once again.

Refining this nautical metaphor, not all boats are in the water. Some are in dry dock awaiting repairs (company restructuring) while some of them are out to sea and leaking. If the fleet is strong, the number of boats under repair and the number that are leaking should be small.

Returning to stocks, some measures of market breadth involve the volume of rising stocks compared to the volume of falling stocks. Rising stocks should be getting the majority of volume in a healthy market. Strength indicators, such as the number of net new 52-week highs (vs 52-week lows), quantify the portion of stocks that are trending higher. Money flow measures the supply and demand for stocks and as economics tells us, greater demand than supply pushes prices higher.

The advance-decline line

Each trading day, the exchange and over-the-counter markets publish statistics on how many of their issues closed higher and how many closed lower. The day's advance-decline for any market is simply the difference between these two numbers. For example, if 1,200 issues advanced and 300 declined, the day's net number would be 900. If 300 advanced and 1,200 declined, the number would be –900. Each day's net number is then added to a running total and the result is plotted in a chart.

If the chart is rising, the advancing issues are dominating the declining issues and the market is then said to be healthy. If it is falling, then the market is not healthy. Most of the time, the advance-decline line and the price of the representative market index move higher and lower together. It makes sense that in rising markets, the majority of stocks should be rising themselves. Conversely, in falling markets, the majority of stocks should be falling.

There are times, however, when the market index is rising while the majority of stocks are falling. Some indices are price or market capitalization weighted in such a way that a few stocks have an influence out of proportion to their numbers. Others, like the Dow Industrial or FTSE focus on a limited number of issues and therefore rely on a limited number of sectors or stocks to determine the market. Usually, these measures are sufficient for most analysis. At other times they may miss the mark to varying degrees.

Fig 12.1 ■ NYSE composite index (top) and advance decline (bottom)

Figure 12.1 shows the New York Stock Exchange composite index (top) and the cumulative advance-decline line (bottom) for 300 days. The chart covers the period leading into the flat market of 1994 that some call a bear market. During the period covered in the chart, the majority of stocks did decline significantly and this is not indicated by the overall market index.

Note the two rising trends highlighted for the index and the corresponding declining trend in the advance-decline line. Both of these divergences correctly forecast the ensuing declines in the index.

Except under extraordinary conditions, the stock market does not turn around instantly. Most of the time markets turn more slowly and more in tune with established business and market cycles. Some market sectors are sensitive to these changes. Others are more independent due to the inelasticity of demand for their products (food, for example). At the end of a bull market, the advance-decline line can roll over and even head lower well before the market indices do. This divergence provides the signal that all is not well and that the market's health has deteriorated.

Conclusion

As with most technical indicators, the traditional stock market advance-decline line works at tops and at bottoms. It applies to many stock markets (New York, NASDAQ, London, Tokyo, etc.) and covers many time frames (daily, weekly) to forecast short-, medium- and long-term junctures. Corrections and reversals work equally well.

The problem is that there is not always a divergence. The advance-decline can only point out unusual conditions but it cannot categorize them by length and severity. Sometimes events happen that cause quick sentiment shifts, such as interest rate changes or political shocks (oil embargo, war, assassinations). Therefore, the advance-decline line takes its place in the trader's toolbox as only one part of a technical team.

Sectors and industry groups

Most of the time, certain sectors of the market are leading the charge while others are lagging. While in a roaring bull market, even the laggards may be rising, too, but you are concerned with putting your money in stocks that will be the best.

The term 'in the right place at the right time' can be applied to stocks just as well as it can to people. Company A may be the low-cost producer of the highest quality newspapers but when the world shifts to the Internet for its news and advertisements, Company A will suffer along with the worst newspaper producers.

Conversely, if Company B manufactures a small component for Internet connections but it is poorly run and suffers many product problems, it will probably be swept along with the global Internet leaders, at least for a while.

This all means that you need to know which sectors of the market are going to lead and which are going to lag. Once you know that, picking stocks from the leaders is a lot less risky.

How do you do that? Fortunately, in most stock markets around the world, there are chartable industry groups available from data vendors. It is easy to find the technical condition of the banks, the food retailers and the computer makers to see which is strong and which is weak. You can then compare their price perform-

> You need to know which sectors of the market are going to lead and which are going to lag.

ance to each other. There will be more on how to do that with relative strength charts later in this chapter.

Volume

The more shares that change hands, the more important the price move. High volume at a support or resistance level makes those levels strong indications of supply and demand balance. High volume breakouts from those levels are key signals of trend and provide high confidence trading points.

Cumulative volume

Cumulative volume (also known as on-balance volume) is simply a running total of daily volume. If the market goes up, then that day's volume is added to the total. If the market goes down, then the day's volume is subtracted from the total. Overlay the result on a simple price chart, something most commercial software packages can do, and supply and demand can be readily seen.

Theory

When bulls are dominating a market, up-days are often accompanied by higher volume than are down-days. The reason is that demand is higher than supply, forcing prices to rise and allowing trades to get done. Whether buyers or sellers were in control on a particular day (or other time frame) cannot be easily seen on simple volume charts. Up-days and down-days within a price trend begin to blur together, leaving only trends in volume visible.

To overcome this, a running total of volume is calculated. Over time, a plot of cumulative volume shows money coming into or flowing out of the market. Rising prices, theoretically caused by higher demand than supply, are usually accompanied by high up-day volume. Conversely, falling prices, theoretically caused by lower demand than supply, are usually accompanied by high down-day volume.

Most of the time, cumulative volume and price move together. However, when the two move in opposite directions, a divergence arises and a trading opportunity is created.

A variation of cumulative volume is also used that weights the volume by the day's change in price. This assigns more weight to the volumes of days with bigger price changes. Both should be used since they do not always signal together but only the unweighted version is used here for simplicity.

Figure 12.2 shows a 300-day chart for Union Carbide. Cumulative volume had been tracking price until the small December 1995 decline. Although prices were falling, cumulative volume held steady, indicating that volume on up- and down-days was relatively even. Bears were not consistently dominating the market and the supply and demand equilibrium had not changed. Prices rebounded by the next month.

In May 1996, the bearish trend halted temporarily as the market moved in a descending triangle pattern. Cumulative volume continued lower even though prices had stabilized. This indicated that bears were still dominating the bulls and that the triangle would break to the downside. The breakdown from the triangle was followed by another six-point loss over the following four weeks.

Note that there was an indication of the likely breakdown in prices due to the descending triangle shape. This type of triangle often points in the direction of the pending breakout and in this case, that was down.

While cumulative volume is most often applied to stocks, any market with volume can be analyzed. Figure 12.3 shows 250 days of US T-bond futures. Note that price and cumulative volume tracked each other until the October–December rally. Prices moved sharply higher but cumulative volume remained flat. This indicated that prices were too high based on the market's buying and selling pressures.

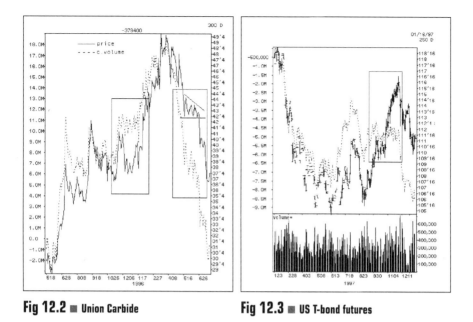

Fig 12.2 ■ Union Carbide   **Fig 12.3** ■ US T-bond futures

The volume histogram chart at the bottom only showed that volume increased as price rose and was a confirming indicator. What it could not show was that volume on the small pullbacks was equivalent to that of the big advances. This is bearish in a rally.

Relativity

Cumulative volume by definition should track price and it does just that most of the time. Like other indicators, trading opportunities are signalled when the two move apart. The rules for using cumulative volume are similar to those for the others.

The most important point to keep in mind is that relative slopes and relative divergences are used. This is because cumulative volume is plotted on a different vertical scale than price. Its shape is also span dependent — a 110-day chart (Figure 12.4) could look different from the same 100 days as viewed on a 300-day chart (Figure 12.5). Cumulative volume could be above price on one chart and below it on the other. However, the directions of the two will be the same as will any trading signal.

Like other indicators, a divergence can last for varying periods of time. Cumulative volume should never be used alone and should always be confirmed by other analyses. It excels as a leading indicator but not as a trading trigger.

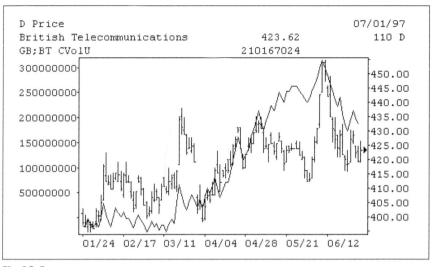

Fig 12.4 ■ **100-day chart**

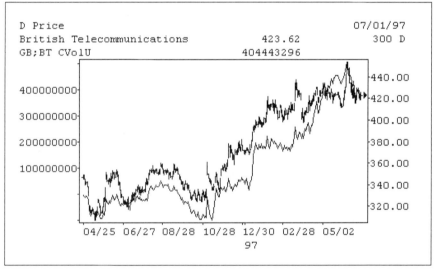

Fig 12.5 ■ **500-day chart**

Momentum

Momentum measurement is the focus of most indicators and seeks to determine how fast prices are moving. Most classic and homegrown indicators revolve around determining stock or market momentum and it is a correct conclusion that all of this interest makes momentum a very important concept. The trend really is your friend and as a certain bullish or bearish feeling gets slowly spread through the market, the trend propagates for identifiable and tradeable periods of time.

Indicators seek to identify trends that are beginning, that are in their prime and that are nearing their end. Most of them are interchangeable for our purposes. There will be more about momentum later.

Divergence

Divergence is the key concept to learn when dealing with supporting studies and indicators. It occurs when the relative trends of prices and of studies are moving in different directions and can be applied to momentum indicators, volume, breadth indicators and even sector analysis. Divergence can be bullish or bearish, depending on the relative directions of the price and studies. Typically, divergences are resolved when the price moves in the direction of the study.

The Relative Strength Index (RSI) is one of the most popular momentum indicators.* In Figure 12.6, the Nikkei index was making lower weekly lows throughout the first half of 1992. In June, the Relative Strength Index (RSI) did not make a lower low. Again, in August, the RSI actually made a higher low. The Nikkei index soon reversed direction and began a six-month rally.

The question to ask is 'How can RSI go up when price is going down?'

Since RSI measures relative strength, which is a form of momentum, an automotive analogy can be used. A car has an accelerator pedal and a brake pedal. If you are driving and step on the brakes for a few seconds, the car slows down. However, unless you step on the brakes with enough force, the car will still move forward. It is the same with a market. Each time selling pressure outweighs buying pressure, the brakes are applied and the RSI goes down a little. Each time buying outweighs selling, the accelerator is applied and the car speeds up (RSI goes up). Eventually, if the brakes are used with greater force than the accelerator, the car will stop. RSI will be trending lower while the price rally will come to an end.

In order for a study such as RSI to predict a possible reversal in trend, look to see if the value of the study reaches an extreme level. In Figure 12.6, the RSI was below 30, which indicated an oversold condition. Typically, below 30 means excessive bearishness (oversold) and above 70 (all on a scale of 1–100) means excessive bearishness (overbought). An oversold market usually stops going down although it does not always start to go up. Use an oversold condition to close out short positions but wait for other indicators to confirm a

---

*The formula for RSI is not important here. Any good software package will have both it and its formula.

buy signal. A divergence in RSI that happens between 30 and 70 is generally not a good divergence indicator.

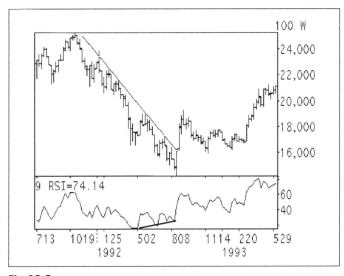

Fig 12.6 ■ Nikkei index

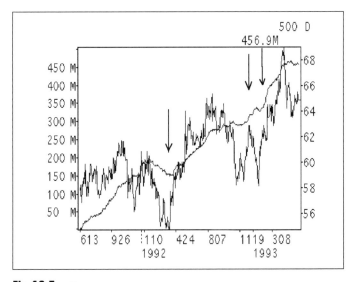

Fig 12.7 ■ Exxon

In Figure 12.7, the money flow (a supply and demand indicator) for Exxon showed a steady increase for the past two years. Analysis of cumulative volume, a similar indicator, can be substituted on charity software that does not have money flow. Throughout the two-year period, the price of Exxon moved significantly away from the money flow line and each time the price of the stock moved back in the direction of money flow. As is evident in March 1992, December 1992 and January 1993, price moved fairly quickly for a fast profit. For divergences in overlays, such as money flow, look for times when the relative direction of the two lines are different. The absolute divergences are not significant, only the relative shapes of the lines.

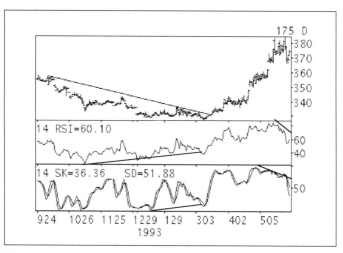

Fig 12.8 ■ Gold

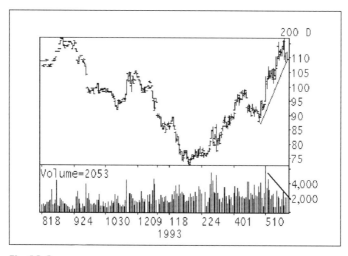

Fig 12.9 ■ Orange juice futures

The gold market in Figure 12.8 broke out of a long-term bear market in March 1993. Both RSI and Stochastics (another momentum indicator) showed higher lows (bullish) from October 1992 until the rally began in March 1993. The lowest low for both studies was below 30. Both studies also showed bearish divergences starting in May 1993 which led to the big sell-off at the start of June. Note that this divergence started earlier in the Stochastic than the RSI. This is because RSI is more reliable in a trending market, but you do not need to worry about the subtle differences between indicators yet.

Volume can also show divergences with price but is a more reliable predictor of market tops than of bottoms. Orange juice futures (Figure 12.9) rallied from January 1993 but while prices were peaking in late May, volume peaked several weeks earlier. Declining volume here indicates that there was less buying pressure for the commodity which then indicates an internal market weakness.

> RSI is more reliable in a trending market.

Time

Time may march steadily onward in defined increments but there is much to be gleaned from it. How much time did the market spend in its trend? Is the small trading range now long enough to allow for the excesses and imbalances built up during the trend to dissipate?

Price cycles emerge from the data when you look for them. Most futures traders use an annual cycle called seasonality. If you are trading corn, you know that supply increases at harvest time and that extreme weather conditions during the growing season may limit supply. There may also be links between corn and livestock prices since corn is used for feed.

Cycle analysis can be complex so will not be covered as part of the main focus of this book. There is more about cycles in Chapter 29.

Sentiment

In any market, whether financial, commercial or consumer, prices are set when supply and demand are in equilibrium. No matter what a favourite technical indicator or fundamental report might say, prices will not move unless the relationship between supply and demand changes. Since individuals' beliefs of fair value are based on expectations of the future, prices at which they are willing to trade change with the prevailing mood in the market.

Sentiment indicators

Sentiment indicators measure the expectations of participants in the market. These participants can be broken down to include individual investors, corporate insiders, stock exchange members, mutual funds, institutional traders, floor traders and newsletter advisory services.

These sentiment indicators are actually measuring the emotions of these investors. As is the case with most things in life, emotions change. They swing back and forth. Sentiment indicators swing back and forth between extremely bearish and extremely bullish.

The majority of investors are usually most optimistic at a market top and most pessimistic at a market bottom. The more optimistic or pessimistic the majority is, generally, the more significant the top or bottom is. Why? When everyone is so bullish, they have already stepped up their buying activity and there are few people left to buy. Without more bulls, the market cannot go up. The converse is true at bottoms when the bears become exhausted.

Market participants who are better informed (the minority of investors) seem to buy and sell in a contrary manner to the majority. When the majority seems to think things are the worst they have ever been and will probably get worse, a small minority is buying. Conversely, when the majority thinks things are great and will only get better is when this small minority is selling. At significant turning points, insiders are usually following a different course than the general investing public.

One very important thing to keep in mind with sentiment indicators is that they confirm the trend up until they become extreme. In other words, the majority is correct during the trend as the bullish or bearish mood can continue to spread to new bulls or bears, respectively.

To recap. You should not sell just because the majority is bullish. The bullish feeling has to be at an extreme.

Measuring expectations that drive markets

Sentiment is the term used for the summation of all market expectations. It ranges from fear and hopelessness to indifference to greed and complacency. At the bottom of a bear market, the expectations of market participants are almost unanimous for lower prices and more financial losses. As a rally begins, some of these participants become hopeful and prices rise off their worst levels. In the middle of the bull market, many players have changed their expectations but not everyone is bullish.

Near the end of the rally, almost everyone is assuming that the trend will continue. More risks are taken and greed becomes dominant. In other words, market sentiment is at a high. When this happens there is nobody left to buy more. Prices can no longer rise since everyone has already bought.

There are many quantifiable technical measurements of market sentiment. They range from comparisons of small vs large players, strong money vs. weak money and even the tone of magazine cover stories. All are based on the premise that the majority is usually wrong at the extremes. Again, in a rising market, this is because the majority has already bought, so there is nobody left to buy more. Demand has dried up and prices must fall.

Major market turning points often follow high-exposure news reports. The media only consider these stories newsworthy when the trend is widely accepted and a majority opinion is formed. Financial markets generally turn shortly thereafter.

Look for magazine covers and front-page newspaper stories concerning the market that have an element of opinion in them. For example, when you see the French general interest newspaper *Le Monde* feature the picture of a bull arrogantly standing over a defeated bear, the end of the rally market is usually near. The same picture in the *Wall Street Journal* would not be quite as important since the Journal is a financial newspaper.

> Major market turning points often follow high-exposure news reports.

There are many other popular methods used to gauge sentiment but they require data that may not be easily obtained by the individual investor. They are also above the level of this book and are better left to one of the many specialized books on the subject. A very brief summary is included below.

Put/call ratio – The more people that take the bet that the market will drop (by buying puts), the larger the majority. Conversely, high call buying means the majority is betting on a rally. In both cases, the market goes against the crowd. It can be found in any major financial news service.

Short interest – This is limited to stocks only but is essentially the same as the put/call ratio. The more people feel that the stock market will go down, the more they sell short. Selling short is the process of borrowing shares of stock to sell now in the hope of buying them back later at a lower price. Short interest rises as the number of people expecting lower prices increases and the fewer bears are left to keep driving the market down. If the market goes up then all of this short stock will have to be purchased back in a hurry and that sends the market up even faster.

Commercial activity – In the commodities markets, commercial players such as gold mining companies, grain processors and oil companies command a very large share of trading volume. These are the hedgers seeking to lay off risk onto the speculators in order to lock in prices. When commercials buy or sell, it is based on legal insider knowledge of the market and is therefore an excellent indication of general market expectations. In the US, the weekly net commitment of traders report isolates who is trading what. It also breaks down large traders vs. small traders.

The commercials tread through the market like elephants compared with the individual investors who scamper like mice. It is wise to follow their lead. Go against them and you could get squashed.

There are many other sentiment indicators, such as mutual fund redemptions and margin debt levels, but the key is that each measures how much risk market participants are willing to take to fulfill their fear and greed. The higher the degree of speculation, the higher the expectation and the more likely a lack of new buyers – everyone has already bought.

13 Fundamental analysis really is technical analysis

If a company has raised its dividends consistently each quarter, the stock should rise. If earnings continue to grow, that is good, too. This seemingly fundamental information certainly sounds like a pair of rising trends to a technician. A rising trend in these underlying factors usually translates into a rising trend in the stock price.

What about bonds? Rising inflation is usually bad news for the bond market. One of the more popular measures of inflation has been the Bridge/CRB index of commodities futures prices. When the CRB rises, it is bad news for bonds in any developed country. This is fundamental analysis. It is also something known as intermarket analysis and is used extensively by technical analysts. The CRB moves inversely with the bond market.

The stock market is affected by interest rates and the bond market.

Look at this from an 'ivory tower' point of view. The stock market is affected by interest rates and the bond market. The bond market is affected by capital flows into and out of the country and the exchange rates for currencies. Capital flows are determined by global business cycles. It makes sense to pay attention to all of this, even if all you want to do is buy an indexed mutual fund. If capital is flowing into the country, then the bond market benefits, interest rates stay low and the stock market has reason to rise.

Intermarket analysis

Globally, all markets are connected, in that stocks are led by bonds that are themselves led by interest rates. Rates are determined by the economy, which takes its cue from raw material prices. While technical analysis of any individual market can stand on its own, intermarket analysis can add another dimension to the process.

In his 1989 book, *The Intermarket Technician*, John J. Murphy made several key observations. He said that all markets are interrelated and that intermarket analysis borders on economic analysis. This is because traditionally non-technical terms, such as inflation and raw materials are used. He also noted that the word 'domestic' is 'largely irrelevant'. This is shown in the shocks that frequently occur in global equities and even in the very existence of foreign exchange.

The major markets

Now take a look at some of the more common intermarket relationships followed today. Figure 13.1 shows the US stock and bond markets leading into the 'crash' of 1987. In the beginning of the chart, the two markets moved up and down together. Note that the bond trend was broken a few weeks before the stock trend in March. Bonds also led the stock breakout to the upside in June.

In July, bonds began to fall again but this time stocks did not. The farther the two markets diverged, the more violent the eventual correction would have to be. On the day of the crash not only did stocks plummet but also the bond market skyrocketed sending interest rates much lower. Both sides of the equation corrected dramatically.

Traditionally, the Bridge/CRB index has been used to gauge inflation and hence analyze the bond market. Logically, if raw material prices were

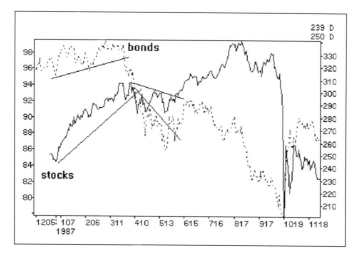

Fig 13.1 ■ US stocks and bonds

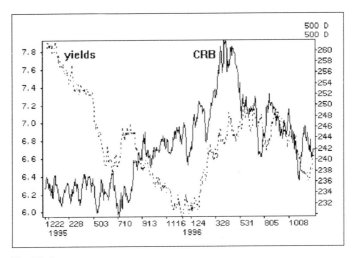

Fig 13.2 ■ CRB and yields

rising, inflation would be at hand and interest rates would also rise. However, this link seemed to have been broken in late 1995 (Figure 13.2). While the dynamics of the global economy may have changed that year, the relationship between the CRB index and interest rates did not. In 1996, the two resumed their closely tied movements.

Figure 13.3 shows the US dollar index against 30-year US bond yields and a clear correlation. Figure 13.4 shows two years of the US dollar index and the CRB index and a clear inverse relationship between the two. The divergence between the CRB index and interest rates in late 1995 is easily explained by the counter-trend move made by the dollar during the same

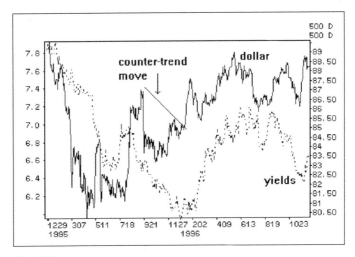

Fig 13.3 ■ Dollars and yields

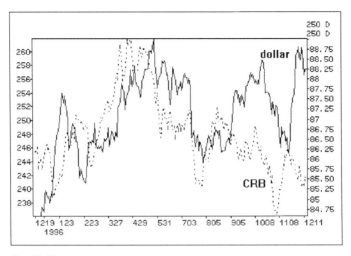

Fig 13.4 ■ **Dollars and CRB**

period. These two relationships help to explain why the CRB-bond relationship was unusual during that time.

Do you need to master these relationships? Certainly not. However, you need to be aware of the big picture so your investments don't get blindsided.

Intramarket relationships

Intermarket analysis can also be applied to similar markets (intramarket). For example, a spread between oats and corn can be used to take advantage of two commodities with some degree of substitutability. Two stocks in the same industry group can be analyzed this way, as well. For example, plot the ratio of one stock to another to measure performance. A stock can also be measured to its industry group or the group to the market as a whole. This is called relative strength analysis and is covered in Chapter 14.

There are times when the market for a specific commodity becomes relatively illiquid and hedging a position is difficult. Canadian cash bond holders used US bond futures to hedge due to the further lack of liquidity in the Canadian bond futures markets.

To tie it all together in a real example, the analysis of a stock, such as chocolate maker Hershey Foods, should include the overall market, its major raw material cocoa, interest rates used to finance operations and debt, and foreign exchange rates used when calculating profits overseas. Any one of these markets affects the shareholders' bottom line.

14 What makes a stock look good?

If you can find at least three of the following characteristics in a stock, the chances are you will pick a winner.

- Rising price trend as more and more investors jump aboard.
- Rising volume as investors become more aggressive in their purchases.
- Strong, but not excessive, price momentum. Anything higher indicates that supply and demand got out of synch.
- Strong sector. If the sector is doing well, there is likely to be enough business for all stocks in it.
- Strong market. A rising tide raises most boats.
- Supportive environment. Low input prices, high output prices, low cost of doing business, favourable supply and demand in the industry.

These are the basic criteria. This chapter examines them a bit more closely.

Trend and momentum

Many technical indicators are trend-following systems that are used to confirm that a change in market direction has already taken place. For example, a moving average turns down after the market peaks because it averages old prices in with recent prices. Momentum indicators, however, are more predictive. They measure the speed of price movements, not the prices themselves.

> Many technical indicators are used to confirm that a change in market direction has already taken place.

If determining the trend is the basic task of technical analysis, then determining its strength is the next step. The momentum of a trend can be measured and its definition when applied to the financial and commodities markets is like its definition in the science of physics. Speed and power determine market momentum. Speed is the slope of the trend. Power is the conviction of the participants as shown by their actions. The former can be measured by all sorts of indicators, most of which are not covered here. The latter can be measured by the volume and, for stocks, market breadth or, for futures, open interest.

It follows that the more people become involved and the more price moves, the more powerful the trend. Of course, it can get ahead of itself. Technicians use the terms overextended or overbought/oversold. No matter what term is used, think of a rubber band getting stretched. Eventually, the forces stretching it are overcome by the forces within the rubber wanting to shrink it. It snaps back and in the markets, this is called a correction.

Momentum defined

When a ball is thrown up into the air its speed (velocity) declines until it stops momentarily in mid-air and then starts to fall. While the ball is still rising, its speed is falling. Markets exhibit this behaviour as well. Determine that the speed of rising prices is declining, and be forewarned that a market top may be near.

For falling markets, another analogy can be used. Take the same ball to the top of a hill and let it go. As it rolls down the hill it gains speed. When it gets to the bottom it is still moving but since the ground is now flat, its speed starts to decline.

These examples help to show that a market will tend to continue in the same direction in which it is moving until some force acts upon it. The rubber ball has forces called gravity and friction, the markets have forces called support and resistance. If a market is moving but does not meet either support or resistance, it will continue to move in the direction of the trend, but at slower and slower speeds until it stops, like a tired long-distance runner. The buying or selling pressures that powered the move have dissipated.

Reading a momentum chart

Most indicators that measure momentum are similar. Some work better for stocks, some are better at market tops, some are better in trading ranges and some are better in trends. For our purposes, they are interchangeable. This will anger established technicians out there but return to the analogy of the car, and you will understand this.

Whether it is a Ford, a Peugeot or a Honda, all cars have an engine. All engines turn fuel into energy that makes the car move. In the markets, all indicators that use price changes and their derivatives measure trend strength and attempt to identify extremes (stretched rubber bands).

There are four basic events to follow on a momentum chart. The *first* is a crossing of the zero line. If momentum is negative and crosses the zero line into positive territory, it could be a buy signal. This is because prices are accelerating their advance as new buyers enter the market. Note that this is only a valid signal when the line is crossed in the direction of the prevailing trend. Trends are still more important than their derivative measure, momentum.

The *second* event is a divergence with price action. If prices make lower lows but momentum makes higher lows, down side market momentum is declining.

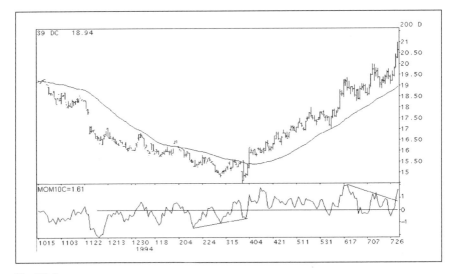

Fig 14.1 ■ NYMEX crude light

Figure 14.1 shows a 200-day bar chart of September 1994 NYMEX crude oil futures with a 39-day moving average and a 10-day momentum indicator. The average serves as a measure of the trend. The 10-day momentum indicator tells us the acceleration of the trend.

In March, while the market was still falling, momentum was becoming less negative. In other words, the speed of the market was declining, even as prices were still moving lower, indicating that selling power was weakening. Note that during the period of divergent momentum, the indicator crossed the zero line several times. Since the trend in the market was down, these zero line crossings were ignored.

In April, the market trend did reverse as prices began to rally. Momentum was in positive territory and settled into a two-month range. Finally, in early June, momentum crossed below the zero line. Since the primary trend was still up, this signal was ignored. Other technical indicators, such as the moving average itself, confirmed this as prices bounced off support.

Later that month, momentum reached a level that was very high as compared to its recent history. This is the *third* event and may indicate an overbought condition where prices got out of line with perceptions. The signal given suggested that the market may need a short rest and that new long positions should not be taken.

Sometimes, when the ball in our analogy above is thrown up, it bounces off the ceiling. In this case, both prices and momentum change at that same time. In this situation, trend breaks in momentum can be useful in place of the first three basic events.

This would normally indicate that the market is near a top, but in late July, momentum broke through its own down trendline (event number *four*) indicating new buying pressures and more gains to be made.

Conclusion

Momentum is a very useful leading indicator but it must be used as an opportunity finding tool, not the final decision-making tool. Confirm all signals with trend breaks and other technical signals, such as reversal patterns on bar charts.

Volume

Volume measures how much money people are putting on the table to back up their bullish or bearish outlooks. The analyst can be bullish or bearish but it is the trader and investor who risk their money. The more money they risk by buying and selling, the greater their convictions must be. We can equate convictions with perceptions and if they rise, so will the market.

According to perceived wisdom, volume should expand during healthy rallies. Expand? That means get bigger. If the market is rising and more and more people are being pulled in to participate, volume will rise.

If the rally is not healthy, such as when the public does not follow the early buyers into the market or when a trend is nearing its end, volume will begin to decline. Fewer people buy smaller amounts and that can be read as a loss of conviction.

During chart patterns that form when the market is taking a rest, volume usually declines. If the market pulls back (prompting the media to label it 'profit taking'), low volume indicates that buyers and sellers are repositioning themselves after the recent rally.

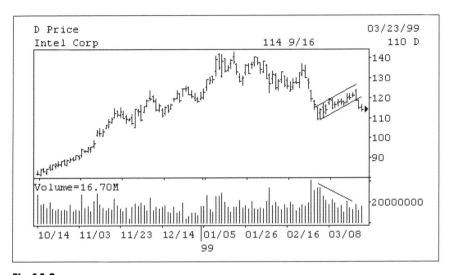

Fig 14.2 ■ Volume

In Figure 14.2 Intel had been trading down from its all-time highs when a rally began in late February. Note that the volume decreased during the rally to indicate that buyers were not attracted to the new low prices, and demand from those still 'buying on dips' was not sufficient to sustain the advance. The stock broke down from the flag in March.

Relative strength (the market, sectors and individual stocks)

Stocks do not exist in a vacuum. How is the stock compared to its industry group? How is the group in relation to its sector? How is the sector positioned against the general market for stocks? Are stocks better than bonds or gold?

When seeking to maximize the probability of a trade's success the investor often starts with a top down approach and moves to specific securities or commodities from there. For example, if the decision to invest in equities as an asset class has already been made, the next question is which equities section will lead the way higher. By comparing the relative strengths of each sector to a common index, the decision can be quantified.

RS is not RSI

Without getting mired in the initials, relative strength (RS) is a measure of how one instrument is performing relative to another. The relative strength index (RSI), in contrast, measures how a single instrument's momentum is changing over time. RSI is a useful tool for making a timing decision but relative strength is better when deciding which instrument to select from a set of favourable candidates.

The formula for RS is a simple ratio of instrument one divided by instrument two and the result is plotted on a line chart. Trendlines, moving averages and other technical tools can then be applied to analyze the plot like any single instrument. The most important aspects of the analysis are trends and trend breaks as shown below.

Fig 14.3 ■ Nikkei vs. Morgan Stanley World Index

Figure 14.3 shows the ratio of the Japanese Nikkei 225 index and the Morgan Stanley world stock index for four years ending in 1996. The latter index represents the global market for equities in general. The long-term trendline indicates that the Nikkei has been underperforming the global equities market for the four years. The intermediate trendline shows that Japanese stocks had been outperforming the world from June 1995 until July 1996. The latter was a counter-trend move within an overall bearish relationship.

Fig 14.4 ■ Nikkei line chart

Keep in mind that the trading pattern for the Japanese market over these four years was a wide trading range (Figure 14.4). If the global equities markets were rising while the Japanese market was flat, the ratio of the two will go down. In mid-1995, the Nikkei rallied at a faster rate than the world so the ratio went up.

Quick visual analysis

Figures 14.5 to 14.10 show the same four-year period for major world stock markets relative to the world index. Quick trendline analysis shows the UK market as represented by the FTSE 100 (Figure 14.6) had broken a trendline to the upside and was therefore suggesting that it would outperform the world for a while. Hong Kong (Figure 14.7) has been matching the world pace for 2½ years and France (Figure 14.8) and Australia (Figure 14.9) are locked in three-year down trends.

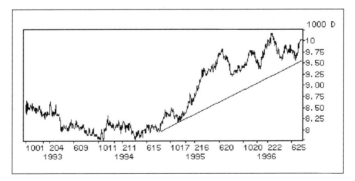

Fig 14.5 ■ Dow Jones/World

Fig 14.6 ■ FTSE/World

Fig 14.7 ■ Hong Kong/World

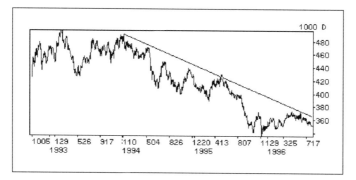

Fig 14.8 ■ France/World

Fig 14.9 ■ Australia/World

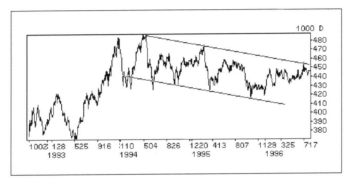

Fig 14.10 ■ Germany/World

Again, this time period has been good for world equities, but relative strength analysis would have helped make the decision of which markets to emphasize and which to de-emphasize in a global equities portfolio.

Basing and breakouts

> Many of the factors that make stocks look good come into play after a trend has been established.

Many of the factors that make stocks look good come into play after a trend has been established. If a stock has been trading quietly in a flat range for a period of time, it may be undergoing a process known as accumulation where the supposed 'smart money' is buying shares. The general public has not caught on to this activity so the price remains stable.

At some point, either through technical analysis, fundamental reports or news events, the stock breaks free from the range. This breakout signals a technical buy signal and the new rising trend is underway. The bigger the base, the stronger the rally can be.

15 Risk vs reward – is this stock really worth it?

Chapter 14 examined what makes a stock a good candidate to buy. This chapter, looks more closely at what makes for a good trade. It is a subtle difference. This is where the monetary potential of a stock is assessed, rather than just its paper prospects.

Think about the difference between doing cosmetic dental work on a child and on an adult. The child's teeth will eventually fall out as the adult teeth grow in. Unless there is a significant health benefit to be gained, the dental 'transaction' will not be worth the costs and possible discomfort. The same is true for a stock. Unless transactions costs and the risk for a loss is zero, you simply cannot buy every stock that passes the tests in Chapter 14. This chapter explains some ways to concentrate on the stocks that have the best chances to make money at an acceptable level of risk.

How can potential profit be measured?

Imagine you have your broker's list of recommended stocks. You also see that one is currently in one of those funny-named trading patterns. As the size and shape of the pattern says something about what the stock might do in the near future, an objective measure can be made of where that stock will go if it breaks out in the right direction.

> The first step in determining where a market is heading is to correctly define the current trading pattern.

Sizing up a pattern

The first step in determining where a market is heading is to correctly define the current trading pattern. The easiest pattern to define is the rectangle, or trading range, because of its uniform size.

In theory, the bottom of a rectangle is the price level at which bulls have decided that the market is undervalued. They are either reacting to changes in market sentiment, as indicated by a break above resistance, or following an existing trend higher. Price moves towards the top of the rectangle where profit taking occurs. This moves the market towards the bottom again as the bears become more active.

At this time the rectangle pattern is not yet evident. Figure 15.1 shows that the MATIF French bond entered a rectangle pattern in July 1991. In this case, the market's decline ended at the bottom of the rectangle where short sellers took profits as bulls decided to buy actively. The market moved higher until new short sellers found a second chance to sell. Again, prices fell to the bottom of the pattern.

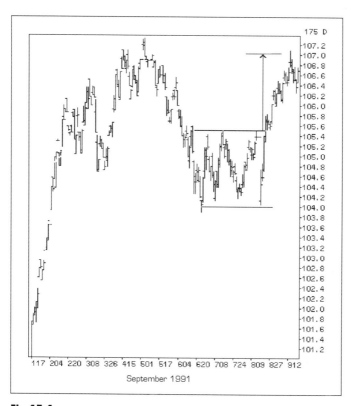

Fig 15.1 ■ MATIF French bonds

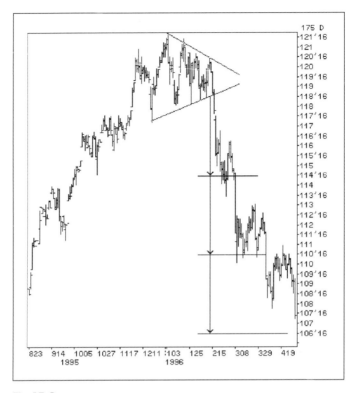

Fig 15.2 ■ US T-bonds

What is different about this bottom is that new buyers had a second chance to buy at the previous low price. It is this cycle of second and third chances that drives the market up and down until finally the market breaks above or below the rectangle. Traders then assume that the old area of value is no longer correct, and in the case of the French bond, the rectangle area was now too cheap.

The rectangle measured approximately 150 basis points (1/100 of a point – the smallest unit of change in this market) from top to bottom. Buyers at the breakout were assuming buying at this new value area would produce a similar profit as it did in the old area. That translated into an upside target of 150 basis points to 107, the top of the rectangle plus 150 basis points equalled 107. This price was reached in a few weeks and proved to be a resistance area.

Coiling patterns

Most patterns require more interpretation than rectangles. For example, a head and shoulders pattern is measured from the neck line to the top of the head. Where the neck line is placed and how much of a tilt it is allowed is up to the analyst.

One pattern that is somewhere in-between these two is the triangle and this includes all variations of the triangle such as wedges, pennants, ascending, etc. A triangle is essentially a trading range that is getting smaller over time (coiling). Sellers do not wait for the previous peak to be reached before selling. Conversely, buyers do not wait for the previous bottom to be reached before buying. This cycle continues until the distance between the highs and lows is relatively small and both sides become unsure of the market's future direction.

Figure 15.2 shows the US treasury bond in a triangle pattern at the end of 1995. This chart appeared earlier, in Chapters 8, as continuation patterns. Here, it is acting as a reversal pattern. The market traded to the triangle's borders several times during that 10-week period so the pattern was well defined. The question is where to measure the height of the pattern.

The best place to measure is at the point of the second border touch. In this case, the second touch is the peak in early January. The distance from that point to the other border can be considered to be the height of the pattern.

Once the market breaks out of the pattern, the pattern height just measured is projected down from the break out point. This becomes the first trading target. For US Bonds, the pattern height was about 4 points. The break occurred near $116\frac{16}{32}$ ($116\frac{1}{2}$) so the first target was $114'16$ ($114\frac{1}{2}$). This level was reached within two weeks and proved to be a support zone.

Integral multiples

The most interesting aspect of pattern projection is that if prices break through the support or resistance supplied by the target price, they often move to a new target that is an integral multiple of the pattern height. US bonds broke through support at $114\frac{16}{32}$ and moved another 4 points to support at $110\frac{16}{32}$ ($110\frac{1}{2}$).

In rare cases, a market can move to a third multiple. However, the third occurrence of many projections, whether multiples of a pattern height or the recurrence of the same pattern over time, often has a variation. In this case, the target was not quite reached. Perhaps the short sellers were covering early, the same way they did in the coiling pattern. In any event, pattern measuring revealed clues as to where the market wanted to go.

Is that a good trade?

When deciding to buy or sell a security or commodity, it is easy to overlook a key component of the trading decision - risk vs reward. If a market is in a bull trend, selling the top of a corrective phase may seem prudent. However, if the downside potential profit is three points, for example, and the upside potential loss if wrong is ten points, the trade simply does not make sense. Technical analysis can help to analyze the risk/reward potential as well as point out immediately when a good trade goes bad.

What makes for a good trade?

A few trendlines on a chart can identify when trading is excessively risky. A weekly chart of the Nikkei 225 index in Japan (Figure 15.3) shows a clear four-year 6,500 point trading range from 14,500 to 21,000. Resistance at the top of the range is very powerful, so selling at that level is low risk. The potential profit is 6,500 points compared to the few hundred points of potential loss if this resistance ceiling is penetrated. If resistance is penetrated, the position is immediately reversed to a buy. With a rectangle pattern, it is not coincidental that the upside profit, once the small loss has been factored in, is still over 6,000 Nikkei points.

Fig 15.3 ■ Nikkei 225 index

A more aggressive approach would be to anticipate a breakout from a consolidation pattern. With this strategy, it is assumed that the pattern will be broken whereas in the above example it was assumed that the pattern will hold. A daily chart of the US dollar/German Mark foreign exchange rate (Figure 15.4) showed an up trend from the October 1995 low. It was caught in a rectangle consolidation pattern but bounced off the longer-term up trendline running through that pattern. The longer-term trendline usually wins the battle against a shorter-term consolidation pattern.

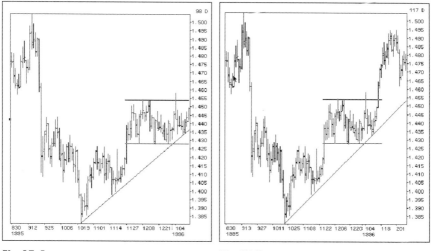

Fig 15.4 ■ Dollar/D-Mark   **Fig 15.5** ■ Dollar/D-Mark later

The result is a risk of 125–130 ticks down to the trendline for a potential reward of 310 ticks as measured by the target for the breakout from the rectangle. In Figure 15.5, it can be seen that this aggressive approach enabled the capture of the entire breakout day. To have waited for the breakout would have lost a large percentage of the total gain.

It's not perfect but it won't kill you

The coffee market is an example of how this approach resulted in a small loss (Figure 15.6). Coffee had been in a down channel since April 1995 (not shown) and finally broke out in January 1996. It moved higher and then settled into a triangle consolidation pattern. A strong momentum indicator (also not shown) plus an unrealized target of 155 based on a projection from the channel suggested a continuation of the rally.

Fig 15.6 ■ Coffee

Buying at the close on 23 February was a low risk way to take a position before the inevitable breakout from the triangle. When the market fell apart in the middle of the next day, crashing through the bottom of the triangle, the trade would have been closed at a 4–5 point loss. When compared to the potential 30 point profit had the market broken the other way, the risk/reward ratio made the trade well justified.

Should you even be playing the game?

Can you stand to take a loss? Can you bounce back if you do? These are important questions you need to answer before you even start to play the investment game.

The key to being able to follow an aggressive, yet low risk, trading approach is to be able to be wrong without going out of business. Taking a 100-point risk to make 300 is a good bet because it enables you to be in the market before the big breakout moves occur for maximum profit. However, if that 100 points of risk will drain 90 per cent of your investment capital, the risk is just too high. You would be better off buying a conservative mutual fund and letting it ride for a few years in an account you never touch.

The saying 'ride the winners and cut the losses' really means that for every big-winning trade, there are several small losing trades.

Sometimes the best trade is the one you don't make

Sometimes the investor has to know when to stay out. Even with the abundance of technical tools available today there are times where the answer to the buy or sell question is simply 'I don't know'. This could be the result of conflicting answers among indicators. It could also be the result of unclear patterns on the charts. In either case, it is often better to stay out of the market and preserve capital for a better opportunity in the future. Consider a few examples where the analysis is unclear.

> Sometimes the investor has to know when to stay out.

No follow-through

In Figure 15.7, soybean oil was trading in a range from October to December 1996. On 9 January, 1997, the market made a strong move higher on very strong volume. This broke the 50-day moving average to the upside. The combination of volume and average was a good buy signal and the next day the market was up on a gap and heavy volume.

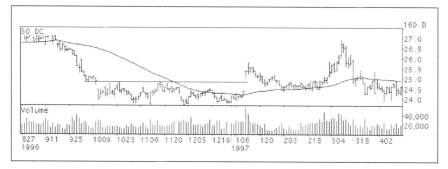

Fig 15.7 ■ Soybean oil

Traders smart or lucky enough to have bought on January 9, were then faced with conflicting signals. Gaps, especially those on high volume, are powerful signals. The penetration of the moving average and move above a technical trading range are also good signals. However, there was no follow-through after the gap. As Chapter 10 showed, a gap can signal either the explosive beginning of a new trend or the exhaustive ending of an old one. While there was no rising trend to end in this case, the lack of follow-through made the breakout suspect.

As can be seen in Figure 15.7, the market did a slow drift lower until it met the 50-day average. Somewhere in that decline, the long position would have been closed, conceding that the trade did not work. Even though the buy signals were correct for a longer time frame, this market may be one to avoid until more solid technical patterns develop.

Erratic behaviour

Sometimes the markets jump around without any apparent rhyme or reason. The foreign exchange charts below exhibit trendline violations, false breakouts and general erratic behaviour.

Figure 15.8 is the Australian dollar/US dollar rate for 325 days. Note the short-lived upside break in September 1996 from an unorthodox flag pattern. In November, the market broke below horizontal support to signal the start of a new declining trend. It reversed immediately. Trend following systems, such as moving averages and even the RSI, were unable to consistently forecast correctly.

In Figure 15.9, the US dollar/Canadian dollar rate is shown weekly for three years. This market reversed course constantly and was especially confusing during mid-1996. Short-term analysis may have worked during that time but position trading was nearly impossible until smooth trends developed in October 1996.

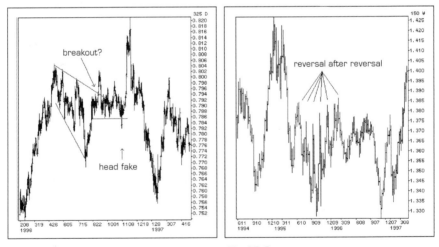

Fig 15.8 ■ Australia/US   **Fig 15.9** ■ US/Canada

Forcing a market into a buy or sell mode is a mistake. The market will tell you what it wants to do. If you do not understand what that is or if the market is telling you that it does not know either, the best trade is the one you do not actually make.

16 This isn't brain surgery

As important as you may think precision is in investing, market analysis of any kind is just not a precise endeavour. Sure, for an arbitrage trader moving millions of dollars, euros or yen around the world, every decimal point is important. But when you are an average investor or even a smaller-scale professional, squeezing that last sixteenth of a point out of your trade of 500 shares does not add up to that much money.

The same thinking can be carried through to the analysis itself. Price patterns or moving averages are still arbitrary, no matter how many computers are used to derive them. The market is a living being and as such, it does not react to the world exactly the same way twice. Nor does it care about | **Flexibility is the key.** how you, the individual human player, classifies its behaviour. Flexibility is the key. If you stick too closely to the textbook definitions, you may be right, but you will also have a lot of losing trades.

Technician's license

The debate continues as to whether technical analysis is an art or a science. Those of the latter belief work with equations, trading systems and models. Those of the former belief use trendlines, traditional technical patterns and an experienced eye. Just like writers who use journalistic licence to bend the rules of grammar and facts, market technicians selectively ignore various chart points, to create a meaningful and, more importantly, useful analysis.

Rationale

Technical analysis has many objective rules and techniques but it all still depends on the subjective interpretations of the analyst. For example, after a market establishes a support level and trades one or two ticks below it, is that considered to be a break of support? What if it traded below support for only a brief time and then bounced right back up? The analyst must use other indicators and rely upon experience to determine if this was a real signal or just market 'noise'.

Strict interpretation of technical rules can cause the technician to set seemingly accurate support and resistance levels that are weak and not related to true market conditions. Figure 16.1 shows 350 days of LME Aluminum. At the 1,740 level, a former support line has turned to resistance. However, it is unclear which exact price should be considered to be significant. The June low is 1,738. In September it was 1,730. In October, the highs were 1,746 and 1,737.

Spending too much time deciding which price to use in a trading system or model can let profitable trades slip away. The line drawn is at 1,738 but can really be represented by a resistance zone of 1,737 to 1,748. By using a single price, extreme intraday reactions can be ignored and this automatically places greater significance on a concensus of several market levels.

Fig 16.1 ■ **LME Aluminum**

The October–November support line is clearer at about 1,655 but that means that at least two bars had penetrated support. These points can be ignored so that one may set up a support line that has been touched five times and is therefore a meaningful level.

Best fit

Unlike regression analysis where a line is drawn to represent all the data, fitting a trading channel to the market places support and resistance trend lines at levels that correspond to the majority of significant highs and lows. Figure 16.1 shows a short-term rising channel in mid-1995 with a technically precise support line (channel bottom) but a parallel resistance line (channel top) that has been violated at least once. The channel top shown touches the tops of the bars on at least three occasions and is much more significant than a channel top drawn through the extreme top in May.

Similarly, the longer-term down-channel of 1995 shows a parallel channel bottom that touches three points while ignoring an extreme low set in February.

Fig 16.2 ■ Orange juice futures

Figure 16.2 above shows 150 days of NYCE orange juice futures. In mid-1995, a long-term down trend was reversed and orange juice rallied in a clear channel. Strict adherence to the rules of trendline construction would have dictated that the supporting trendline be drawn from the market bottom through the first significant retracement (correction). That trendline, shown dotted, would be essentially meaningless. By using the next significant low as the start of the trendline, not only can a meaningful trend be identified but also a resisting channel top can be added to contain the rally. Note here too, the channel top was violated by an extreme trading range day but it still touches price action a significant number of times.

Let the market talk

Most technical analyst beginners, and probably a few experienced ones as well, look at a chart with preconceived notions about what the market will do. This usually narrows the analysis and often provides incorrect results. The theme for this section is, 'you cannot impose your will on the market.' The market will always tell you what it is doing. The secret of technical analysis is to wait for the market to talk before trading and continue to listen in case it changes its mind.

Finding order

Some charts, like those of the major stock markets, seem to travel up or down for long periods of time. Finding the trend there is easy.

Figure 16.3 shows a portion of the long trend in the US stock market interrupted in 1994 by a well-defined triangle consolidation pattern. A breakout from the pattern gave a very obvious signal. Late in 1995, a small down flag occurred followed by a push towards new highs.

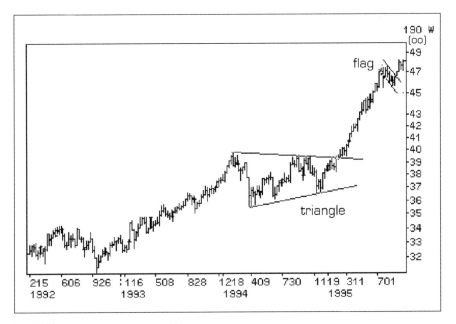

Fig 16.3 ■ **Dow Jones 30 industrials**

The Australian dollar, Figure 16.4 moved higher and lower against the US dollar for seven years, so finding a relevant trend is a little more difficult. The first thing to do is to find short, medium, and long-term trends. From 1989 to 1993, the decline in this market was resisted by a well-defined trendline (A). When it was broken to the upside in 1994, a new long term trend began (B).

However, the supporting trendline was broken in 1995 as the market fell from 0.77 to 0.71. Looking back, the 1994 rally could be considered a medium-term rally within an overall long-term up trend.

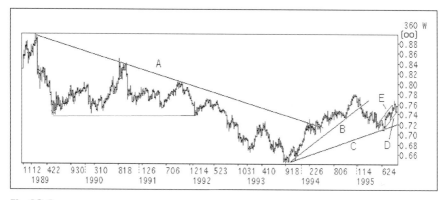

Fig 16.4 ■ Australian/US dollar

This really cannot be determined with reasonable certainty until the market breaks the 1994 high, thereby validating the new long-term up trendline (C).

Making a trading decision

Given that the market is an intermediate-term rising trend, the next step is to determine support and resistance. A long-term support-line can be drawn from 1989 and early 1992. The intermediate up-trendline from the 1995 lows (D) sits at 0.7470 after successfully supporting the rally several times. Both trendlines (C) and (D) provide bullish support.

The next step is to determine the next major resistance level. This establishes a likely price target, which is critical in determining the risk/reward scenario. Should the major resistance be only a short distance away, it would be prudent to wait for that level to break rather than risk that it does not break. The latter event could send the market down to major support and a significant loss.

Resistance is relatively easy to spot as the late 1994 highs near 0.778. Confirmation comes from the top of an intermediate trading channel (E), which will cross that peak in the near future. When a trading channel bottom successfully holds, the likely price target is the top of the channel.

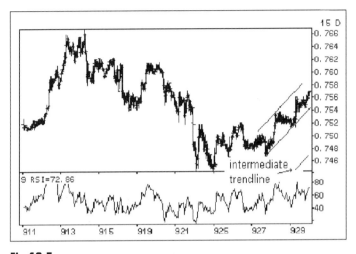

Fig 16.5 ■ Australian/US dollar hourly

The final step is determining your own trading horizon. A position trader, who holds a position for several days to several weeks, might buy at this point. A day trader or short-term trader would look at a shorter time frame, such as hourly (Figure 16.5), to find the best entry point. The chart shows that RSI has fallen somewhat and the market has traded sideways from the channel top to the channel bottom twice already during this short-term move. It might be better to wait until the market reaches the channel bottom before buying. In fact, a break of this channel might actually become a short-term sell signal within the intermediate-term rally.

Summary

The market reveals many things as the data are manipulated through various times frames and spans. Once the overall direction of the market can be found, trading decisions can be made in line with your own trading style. The secret is to let the market talk. If you have difficulty finding trends, it is better not to trade than to force trendlines and patterns onto the chart. The market often does the opposite of what you would expect.

Let the market talk.

Theme and variation

Technical analysis has always been considered an interpretive skill and often cannot be tamed by mechanical systems. Even the latest innovations in setting trendlines and price targets cannot substitute for the human mind in leaving room for variations of traditional patterns. Consider a familiar price pattern in several different ways.

Head and shoulders standard

Most technical patterns can be applied to up and down markets with equal reliability. Here the example is a rising market. In 1995, the wheat market (Figure 16.6) was making a series of higher highs and higher lows, a classic indication of a bull market. In August, the market made a low at about the same level as the previous low and also failed to rally back to a new high. This failure to make a higher high is the first indication that a head and shoulders reversal pattern is in progress. To review, the highest high is called the 'head' and the two peaks on either side are called the 'shoulders'. A line connecting the corresponding lows is called the 'neck line' and provides support for the pattern.

Fig 16.6 ■ The wheat market

In a simple head and shoulders pattern, the market should trade down from the top of the right shoulder towards the neck line. If the neck line is penetrated, the reversal pattern is completed and the market should move lower. If the neck line support level holds, then the market should continue higher as the reversal pattern failed to complete. The wheat market bounced off the neck line area several times before it resumed its rally, forming a complex form of a right shoulder. The rising trendline provided further support.

The failed head and shoulders pattern in this case allowed the market to work out the overbought condition caused by the accelerated June–July rally. Wheat then resumed a slower, but more sustainable, longer term rally.

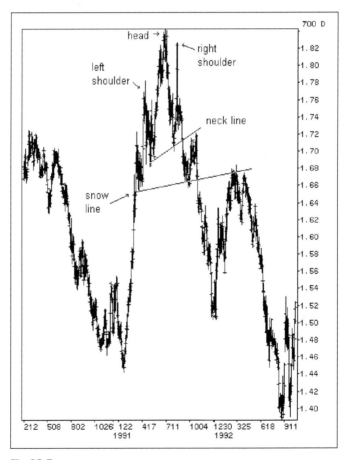

Fig 16.7 ■ US dollar/D-Mark

(Note that the June–July rally, 'the head', ended with a smaller, yet success-ful, head and shoulder reversal.)

Multiple body parts

While wheat displayed a complex shoulder, it is not uncommon for a mar-ket to display a multiple shoulder, or even a multiple head. The US dollar-German Mark exchange rate (Figure 16.7) was making higher highs and higher lows during its 1991 rally until a head-and-shoulders pattern com-pleted in September of that year. The market made a lower low and lower high after the neck line broke which confirmed that a small bear market was in progress. However, the two peaks on either side of the head formed a pattern that also looked like a larger head-and-shoulders pattern sur-rounding the original pattern.

This can be called a mountain top pattern to differentiate it from a simple head and shoulders. The neckline in this case can be called the 'snow line', which completes this analogy.

Since dollar/Mark was already trading lower, this mountain top pattern did not serve to confirm or deny the current trend. However, when meas-ured like a standard head and shoulders (top of head to the neck line), it projected the first target for the decline. The snow line also served to resist the early 1992 bounce rally.

Subjective and interpretive

Analyzing multiple heads or shoulders, and even the different numbers of bars needed to complete these patterns, depends on the skills and experience of the analyst. While mechanized pattern recognition programmes are useful, their learning abilities (artificial intelligence) cannot yet interpret the subtle and not so subtle violations and exceptions common in the real world.

In the real world, nothing is textbook, so stay flexible

Technical analysis is based on the premise that price patterns repeat them-selves. This is because people in the markets repeat themselves given simi-lar market conditions. Unfortunately, in the real world, the term 'similar market conditions' is sub-ject to interpretation. Studying one market as it trends and reverses shows how much leeway there is in a technical pattern and what to do when things 'sort of' happen.

> Technical analysis is based on the premise that price patterns repeat themselves.

When things 'sort of' happen – a case study

The US 30-year bond yield was in a downtrend starting in early 1992. Figure 16.8 shows that for much of 1993 to date, the yields had been in a tightening trading range centered at 6.9 per cent. An upward sloping triangle pattern was emerging and the momentum indicator under the price chart had broken down through its own up trendline.

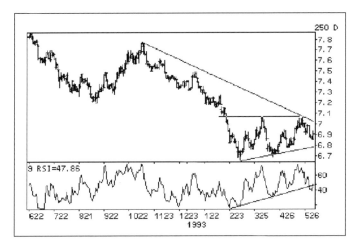

Fig 16.8 ■ T-bond yields

In looking at this chart, the first thing the analyst should do is draw the down trendline from the November 1992 peak. Next, the triangle pattern should be drawn connecting the market bottoms in February and April (using a little technician's licence). The top of the triangle is a clear horizontal line at 7.07. Here, the observation is that the triangle top and the November down trendline meet at a local market reversal to the down side. Since triangle patterns generally are continuation patterns, the evidence points to a down side break of the triangle and a continuation of the declining trend.

Figure 16.9 shows the next three months of trading. In early June, the market broke the triangle pattern and continued its decline. Here, the observation is that the new short-term trend is much steeper than the longer-term trendline. Seven months earlier, this same situation occurred and the market responded by consolidating into the triangle just analyzed. In early July, there was a small correction but it did not take prices back to the trendline. The likely target was the longer-term trendline and since it was not reached, this trade would have produced a small loss.

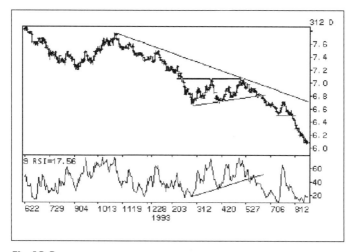

Fig 16.9 ■ T-bond yields 2

From that point on, the only way to trade this was to stay with the trend. Finally, in October 1993, the chart showed a bullish divergence between the falling price and the rising indicator, giving the signal that a bottom had been reached. It is interesting to note that this bottom pattern can be classi-fied as an imperfect double bottom (see Figure 16.10).

When the short-term trendline was broken in November, the buy signal was given and once again the target could have been presumed to be the longer-term trendline. When yields reached that line, they stalled and traded in a narrow range for several weeks. Since momentum was neutral, the investor had to wait for the next signal for direction and that would have been a breakout from the imperfect rectangle pattern indicated.

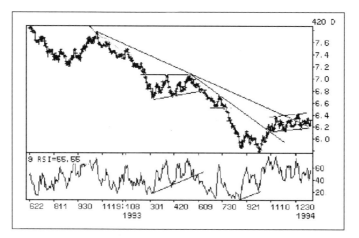

Fig 16.10 ■ T-bond yields 3

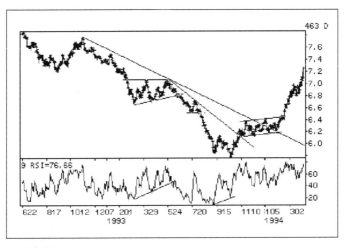

Fig 16.11 ■ T-bond yields 4

In Figure 16.11, yields broke to the upside and established a strong upward trend.

Conclusion

Many of the patterns examined in this chapter were imperfect and, based on the time frame of the analysis used (daily over several months), some losses were produced. This is a much more likely scenario in the markets than any textbook case. The key is to be able to recognize a wrong trade early and to see the bigger picture of the long and short term together. Technical patterns are rarely crystal clear because some market participants do not wait until they complete before acting. This forces patterns to distort slightly even though the general meaning is not changed.

part

4

The actual process of investing

17 OK, now do it!

Day traders and long-term investors have many differences resulting from their different time horizons (investment horizons). Technical analysis may tell the former to sell and the latter to buy, but the one thing they have in common is the act of trading. In order to execute their strategies, whether they be long- or short-term, each has to put their analysis into action. The simple act of 'pulling the trigger' to trade is the final step.

The questions

Once all charts have been marked up with trendlines, studies and other technical tools, the technician needs to set the final criteria needed to trigger a trade. These factors include target price for a winner, stop price for a loser and price at which the trade should be executed. The opinion on a particular stock or commodity may be bullish, for example, but there are several questions that you should consider.

- What is the ratio of profit potential to loss potential at my target and stop prices?
- Am I trading with or against the trend of the next longer term?
- Should I trade at the current market price or wait for a better execution price level?

The first two are easy to answer if the preceding analysis was complete. The third question is harder in the subjective world of trading. The answer depends on the timing of the analysis. If the technical breakouts or reversal signals have already been made, then it may be too late to trade that particular signal. It might be better to wait for the first correction before trading.

If these signals are about to happen (based on the analysis) then it may be too early for all but the most aggressive trader. However, if the signals have just happened, the best way to trade is usually at the market. We can assume that this last case will be the most relevant to the trader or investor who follows the market regularly.

No fear

Once targets and stops are set and the trading signals are given, the technician can execute the trade with no fear. Losses are limited and projected profits should make the risk of these losses worthwhile. In general terms, if the profit potential is at least three times the loss potential, the trade is worthwhile. Keep in mind that like baseball players, traders who can win 40 per cent of the time are leaders in their profession. The value of the six losers is far outweighed by the value of the four winners.

> Traders who can win 40 per cent of the time are leaders in their profession.

The Nikkei index in Figure 17.1 was in a significant bear market going into the start of 1997. After falling nearly 2,000 points in one week, it began a rising triangle-shaped correction that lasted until late February when the index broke down. Short-term traders should have sold early in the day during the big drop on 28 February. Long-term traders might have waited until the close to sell but it is worth examining why it was still a prudent trade.

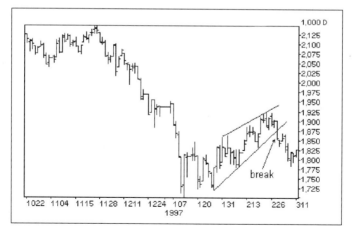

Fig 17.1 ■ Nikkei index

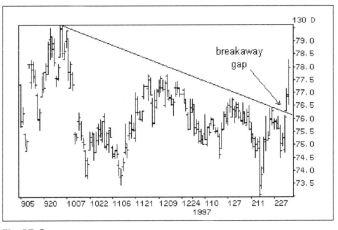

Fig 17.2 ■ Cotton futures

Technical analysis showed that the long-term trend was down. The wedge size suggested a downside target of 17,550* and a reasonable stop level was the 18,875 resistance level seen throughout February. The close on 28 February was 18,557 so the profit target was roughly 1,000 points. The loss at the stop price was just over 300 points. This is a better than 3–1 ratio and hence a good risk.

Cotton futures in Figure 17.2 broke above a descending triangle on 7 March on a small gap up. This should have immediately triggered a buy order at the close. The following day, the market gave back a few points in the morning before exploding higher. Failure to assess the risk/reward of the trade and then acting could have cost the technician the entire 100-point profit of the following day. The risk was essentially getting stopped out just below the trendline for a loss of no more than 75 points (ticks). Considering the size of the triangle, the profit potential was approximately 550 points.

This brings us to the scenario of late analysis. What if you did not know about the breakout in cotton for a few days? At that point, you will need to determine if the remaining 450 points of profit are worth the now 175 points of risk. This time, the ratio is below 3–1 so it might be better to wait for a pullback, reassess the trade and then decide.

If you decide that the market is still going up, the best thing to do is set a closer stop, that is, the price cotton has to fall to prove you wrong and get you out. While the stop price was originally set by a support level, this new stop can simply be a percentage or set number of points below the trade price. Wherever the stop is set, it serves to improve your risk/reward ratio by limiting your losses.

———————
*See Chapter 15.

To round out this section look at a losing trade and see that pulling the trigger to exit a trade is equally as important as it is to enter a trade. In Figure 17.3, the spot Australian/US dollar exchange rate broke below its technical support on 7 November. This should have triggered a sell order. However, the next day, the market reversed, sending the pair back above the former support level; the predetermined stop price. The trade should have been stopped out immediately. In the three weeks that followed, prices soared.

The lesson here is that action must be taken and as long as risk and reward are properly assessed, the probability of making 60 per cent losing trades should not be feared.

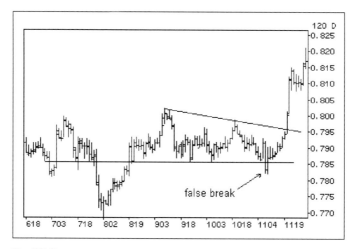

Fig 17.3 ■ Australian/US dollar

18 How to know if you are wrong

Invalidating a trendline

As covered in Chapter 7, prices can briefly penetrate the boundaries of technical patterns without invalidating them. Usually when this happens, prices snap back within a period or two. Volume and momentum studies can help determine whether the violation was significant or not, but they still depend on how strong the pattern or trendline was and how much power the market had when it broke through. If either the pattern or the breakout were weak, it may become necessary to adjust the trendline or boundary to include the new data.

Changing a line

The more a trendline is touched by prices, the stronger it becomes and the more significant a breakthrough it will be. Small violations of the trendline may simply mean that the original line was set too tightly and should be adjusted to include the new data.

> The more a trendline is touched by prices, the stronger it becomes.

The US dollar/Canadian dollar exchange rate (Figure 18.1 – hourly data) shows at least seven occasions where prices rallied to the medium-term trendline without breaking through. On 27 March, prices finally moved above the line, supported by the short-term rising trendline. Volume was light on that day and trading over the next two days was more sideways than trending. The medium-term trendline was adjusted to capture 28 March trading. On the next day, the market proved this strategy correct as it plummeted from the trendline to break the short-term trend and establish new lows (Figure 18.2).

Fig 18.1 ■ US/Canadian dollar   **Fig 18.2** ■ US/Canadian dollar

Time breaks

When a technical pattern, such as a triangle, breaks, prices begin to trend in the direction of the break. The typical conditions for a valid break are a significant price move on an increase in volume. A significant price move is one that is relative to the specific market and not just a few ticks. Triangles have another condition and that is that the prices break out at approximately ⅔ of the triangle length (see Figure 18.3). It shows that the pattern was broken close to the apex where the upper and lower boundary lines meet. Breakouts must be due to price movement, not the passage of time, with the latter occurring simply because the triangle ran out of room.

Now that the triangle is invalid, the remaining unbroken trendline may gain added significance. In the case of gold, the lower boundary was still a valid supporting trendline. However, if a triangle pattern occurs in isolation and not as part of a longer-term formation or trend, both boundaries must be ignored.

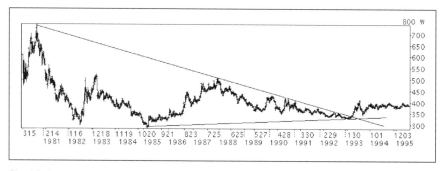

Fig 18.3 ■ Gold

Art and science

While quantitative methods have their place in technical analysis, trader experience and judgment still play a key role. As long as greed and fear rule the markets, rules for trendline and pattern construction can be broken, at least temporarily, without changing the outcome of a trading decision.

Remember that the secret is to be flexible in your application of indicators and flexible in their interpretation. Let the market talk but ignore the accent.

Sometimes being wrong is good

Most of the time, the technical trader or investor identifies a chart pattern and then waits for a breakout higher or lower. However, the market often gives advance warning about its intentions within these patterns, allowing the aggressive trader to capture additional profit with an early trade.

Failure that forewarns

When a market is trading in an identifiable pattern, such as a flag, rectangle or channel, it moves from the top of the pattern to the bottom repeatedly. The more often prices touch these borders, the stronger the pattern and the more significant the eventual breakout will be. If the market has developed an underlying strength, prices often fail to trade back down to the lower border. This failure, when combined with other bullish technical indicators, suggests that the direction of the breakout from the pattern will most likely be up and that it should occur the next time prices approach the top border.

Figure 19.1 shows 200 days of daily data for the FTSE 100 index. The rally from July 1993 paused to correct twice that year, each time in a flag formation. The second correction, which started in October, showed a very clear pattern where prices failed to trade to the lower border in late November. A momentum indicator (not shown) was rising and prices broke through the top of the pattern with considerable force.

Markets sometimes trade in ranges for long periods of time. In fact, some long-term analysts find stocks or commodities trading in identifiable rectangle patterns for years. When these analysts find failure in the charts, their clients have ample warning to analyze both technical and fundamental information to make very high probability trading decisions. Even traders with shorter time horizons can see the signs that an otherwise 'boring' market is about to wake up.

The Nikkei index (Figure 19.2) was locked in a three-month trading range starting in June 1994. In early August, prices failed to reach the bottom of the rectangle but indicators such as Stochastics (not shown) did not confirm this. Later in the month, prices failed to reach the top of the pattern and that time, Stochastics confirmed the failure. Remember, successful technical trading and investing demand that any signal be confirmed by other indicators, the more the better.

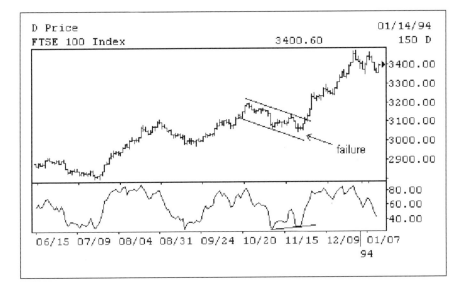

Fig 19.1 ■ FTSE

Fig 19.2 ■ Nikkei

Failure that cuts losses

Earlier in the pattern, in late July, the Nikkei exhibited another kind of failure. Prices broke down below the support line of the rectangle, which signalled many traders to sell. However, the very next day prices scored a one-day reversal pattern and closed back within the rectangle. This failure to maintain the breakout signalled to all traders who sold the previous day that they were wrong and that their short positions should be closed with a small loss.

Even more complex patterns can show failure. A head-and-shoulders formation, normally a reversal pattern, completes when prices break through the neckline. The pattern that developed in corn futures in April and May of 1994 (Figure 19.3) was forecasting an eventual rally. However, when prices reached the neckline, instead of breaking through to the upside, they failed and headed lower. Traders who anticipated the breakout higher knew immediately that they were wrong and that purchases should be sold.

In June, corn rallied toward the neckline once again but failed to even reach it at all. This failure was the advance warning that the market was weak and it was confirmed by several indicators. The market broke down from there.

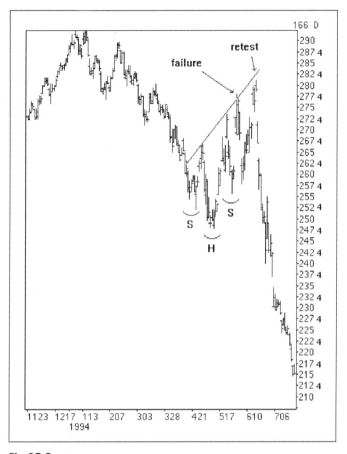

Fig 19.3 ■ Corn

Summary

Trading with failure can provide advance warning for a move to give aggressive traders an additional profit opportunity. It also lets the traders know when they are wrong quickly, to minimize losses. Like all technical trading indicators, confirmation from other technical indicators is the key to understanding the market's true intentions.

> Confirmation from other technical indicators is the key to understanding the market's true intentions.

Note that Figure 19.4 is the same corn chart we saw in Figure 19.3. The only difference is in the markings added. In this case, a flag continuation pattern was drawn. The meaning was the same. It cannot be stated enough — be flexible in your interpretations and open minded enough to adapt to the market.

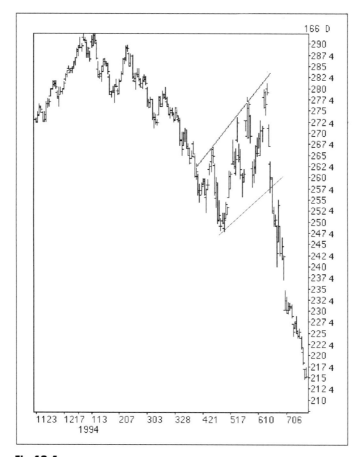

Fig 19.4 ■ Corn

20 When to sell

Most lectures and publications on any investment technique focus on the initial trade. For stock investors, that means the initial purchase. For futures or options traders, that could mean the initial short sale, as well. Not only does this present only half the story, it theoretically sets investors up to lose a good chunk of profits, if not the original invested capital.

For this reason, this chapter ties together other concepts covered earlier and looks at achieving profit objectives. We know when to get out when we're wrong. Now let's figure out when to get out when we're right.

The trend is at its end

This is one of the hardest tasks in the professional investment world. How can the average investor pick tops and bottoms?

This cannot always be done. What can be done is to use technical tools to find reversal signals, trendline breaks and penetration of support/resistance levels, then build a case for continuing to hold the stock or starting to take some money off the table by selling.

There are a few subjective measures to be applied.

- Are you satisfied with the profit made already? In other words, has the stock or market reached your price objective? There is an old adage that states 'Bulls make money, bears make money, pigs get killed.' Do not let greed displace good analysis.

- Has the stock or market simply stopped rising? Sideways action will form one of many patterns on the chart and these patterns can yield clues as to the next move. Many investors would not want to suffer the ups and downs of a choppy market when there are other stocks still moving in strong trends.

■ Has the price rise changed the risk/reward ratio unfavourably? This ties in with the profit objective point above. For example, imagine that you bought a stock with a profit objective of 10 points and a risk of 3 points. It then rises 8 points so you will need to see if the remaining reward of 2 points does not come with a new downside risk that was not evident earlier. This could be changes in the overall market, development of a chart pattern in the stock itself, news, or changes in a related market (such as interest rates or crude oil). Again, just because the chart shows a textbook pattern, breakout and rally does not mean that the price objective will be met. Targets are probable, not guaranteed.

Momentum is down and the market is out of gas

Like a living being, the market can also get tired. Even though it is making further gains or losses, the speed at which it is moving can slow down. This shows up in the charts in many ways.

Divergence

This has already been covered. When prices are rising but the rate and/or power of the rally declines, the bulls are losing their conviction. Momentum indicators, such as the RSI, measure the speed of the rally. If the speed decreases, it means that the bulls are not bidding up prices as aggressively. Likewise, if volume, and hence public participation, decreases, the power behind the rally will not be enough to sustain it.

> Volume measures the power behind the rally.

Sectors

Sectors in the market naturally take and relinquish market leadership as the business cycle matures. Some sectors are early leaders as economic activity develops. Some drive the mature economy. Others excel when the cycle begins to wane. Analysis of sectors can help to determine where we are in the business cycle but this is beyond the scope of this book.

However, sector analysis does provide simpler insights into the health of the stock market. If only a few sectors are driving the major averages higher, then the broad market is not healthy. Focus on the leading sectors, but be forewarned that the general market could deteriorate further. This could take the healthy sectors with it.

The S&P Automobile group was outperforming the market for months until late May 1994 when it broke its relative trendline to the downside (See Figure 20.1.) This signalled that the group was about to underperform the general market and the money should have been shifted away from it.

Fig 20.1 ■ S&P Automobile group relative to the S&P 500

Breadth

Breadth is usually the term given to the participation by individual stocks rather than participation by investors. At the end of a trend, leadership often gets concentrated in a few sectors or individual stocks. Breadth indicators such as the advance-decline line, net new highs and cumulative up-down volume begin to diverge from the major averages. (See Figure 20.2.)

Fig 20.2 ■ Advance-Decline vs. NYSE Composite Index

Unusual news or market conditions cause a shock

The bottom line is that stocks should go up when good news is released and go down when the news is bad. This is a subjective area because not only do you need to classify news or events as good or bad but you also have to decide if the stock reacted to it appropriately.

Stocks that do the unexpected are telling you something. Consider a stock that has been moving higher for weeks going into earnings season. When the numbers are released, they are good, meeting analysts' expectations yet the stock sells off several points. Why? The answer is that people were buying the stock on the expectation that the earnings would be good. The expression 'buy on rumour, sell on news' covers this phenomenon.

Why is this? Stocks drop on good news when the news is either not good enough (expectations were too high) or everyone who wanted to buy has already done so (lack of new demand). If they break lower from a technical pattern on the good news, it is probably a very good time to sell them. The converse is true for bad news and an upside pattern break. (See Figure 20.3.)

Fig 20.3 ■ American Online

Unusual market conditions, such as a collapse in another market or major shift in inflation, can also send stocks moving. One good example is the 1991 Gulf War. Stock markets around the world began an explosive *rally* when war was declared. What could be worse for business in a global economy than war? Customers become enemies, supplies are diverted to the war effort and workers are taken away. (See Figure 20.4.)

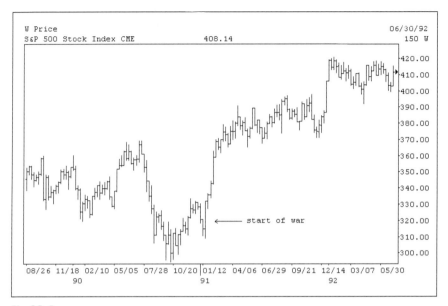

Fig 20.4 ■ **S&P 500**

In this case, all of the news about bad economic times for the world due to the sharp rise in energy prices, among other factors, had already sent stocks lower for weeks. Pessimism was everywhere. The release of all this tension when the war started and people outside of the war zone realized that their economies were really all right sent stocks skyrocketing on the seemingly bad news.

Sudden and unusual rally

Sometimes you own a dream stock. You get in at a low price and all of the sudden, it makes a parabolic rise. What happened? You may have bought it based on a technical breakout, solid rising trend or increase in demand, so you know it was not entirely luck that you made money.

Technical analysis will not provide the answer in all cases so it is important to keep an eye on news events, market conditions or outright speculation by investors.

Something happened to force the market up and this is the time when you consider emotions of the market participants and a wide margin between reality and perception (meaning the fundamentals and market price). Whatever the cause, chances are your momentum indicators are telling you that the market has gone too far, too fast and it is at risk of a break down.

Remember that phrase 'buy on rumour, sell on news'? When the facts come out or the bubble is burst, the stock will come tumbling down. You need not be greedy since you have already made a nice profit.

In Chapter 15, we examined risk and reward. If you own a stock that has gone up 50 per cent in a short time, your risk of the stock falling is probably greater than the reward of another 50 per cent rise. Technical analysts like to catch the major move and most will avoid trying to pick tops and bottoms.

If your stock keeps going up after you sell, so be it. The risk/reward ratio was not favourable. The rally from there simply beat the odds. Even the long-shot horse comes in first once in a while.

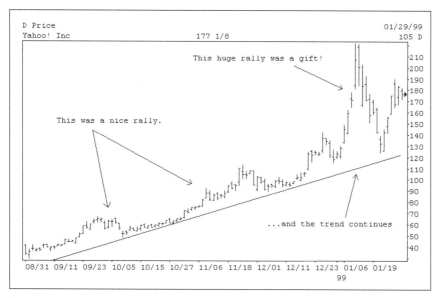

Fig 20.5 ■ Sudden and unusual rally

To recap:

■ Your selected stock makes a sudden or very big run.

■ The risk/reward ratio has changed for the worse.

■ Indicators may flash warnings that momentum or demand has diminished.

■ Perceptions have moved away from reality so any negative news or change in the market will cause heavy selling.

> **You are in the game to make prudent investments, not speculative gambles.**

The odds of continued success have become too great. Even if the stock continues to go up 20, 50 or 100 per cent after you sell, remember that it is a rare occurrence. You are in the game to make prudent investments, not speculative gambles. 'Bulls make money, bears make money, pigs get killed.'

Reversals

Reversal patterns are excellent indications that the trend is in jeopardy. A simple reversal pattern, such as a one-day reversal, can be the first event in the transition from bull to bear market. Trends may remain intact, support still holds, but something happened to cause the bulls to lose their desire and allow the bears to take over. It could be an earnings report, a strike at an assembly plant, a lawsuit or simply the remarks of a widely followed analyst. Whatever the catalyst, the result is a shift from the bulls to the bears.

Of course, the larger, more complex reversal patterns that develop over time are better signals. They give ample warning that something has changed with several opportunities to sell before the market drops.

Volume spikes

Volume is an essential tool in any market. Like other indicators, trends and divergences in volume can yield clues as to pending market actions. However, unlike derived indicators, single-period data can have significant meaning. When a stock or futures contract suddenly trades a significant multiple of its average volume, something important usually has or is about to happen.

Breakouts

The most common use of sudden high volume is as a confirmation of a technical breakout. A real world example can be found in the chart of Oracle Corp in Figure 20.6. A mid-December 1996 volume spike occurred as price gapped down through a supporting trendline. The stock languished for several weeks at the previous support level of 27 ¼ but the high volume gap had changed the dominant trend.

Also on the chart is an earlier gap above the small July-August slides it, too, took place on high volume but not at a subjectively high enough multiple. This was a break of a consolidation, not a change in primary trend. The later March 1998 gap up was not accompanied by unusually high volume since average volume had peaked months earlier.

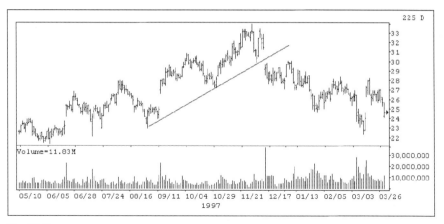

Fig 20.6 ■ Oracle

Buying climaxes

A selling or buying climax occurs after a long down or uptrend respectively when both price and volume spike. Price reaches a new extreme on a big move while volume rises dramatically. In a rally, this represents the final buying frenzy and signals the exhaustion of buying pressures that created the trend.

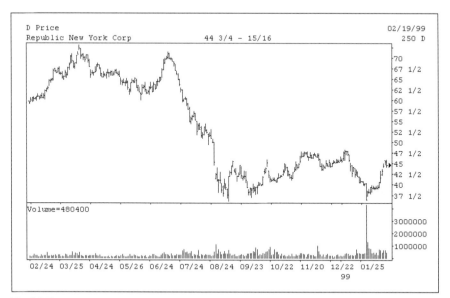

Fig 20.7 ■ Republic New York

In Figure 20.7, Republic New York was moving lower at the end of a long decline. The trend accelerated until the final big sell-off day and high volume. This proved to be the bottom.

Price objective is reached

When a profit target is reached, it is often a good time to sell. This must be balanced against the adage 'Let your profits ride' which suggests that you only sell stocks when they start to go down. A better strategy would be to reevaluate the entire situation to see if technical indicators continue to point to higher prices. If they do, set a new target as well as criteria for what has to happen to prove you wrong.

Stop is hit

A stop price is an automatic order to buy or sell a security at a predefined price. Some trading systems or trading models may use buy stops in the stock market to enter the market on a pattern breakout. Most non-professionals use stops mainly to sell a stock that has gone down instead of going up.

For example, if a stock is purchased at a price of 50 with a target of 65, a stop of 45 might be used. This could be the break of a support level, a simple percentage below the original purchase price or an acceptable risk given the potential reward. In all cases, the losses are limited.

Selling at a stop price takes the emotion out of the decision. The stop itself is a clear indication that you were wrong to buy. Do not hesitate. Cut your losses now! Professionals who have continuous real-time access to the markets may use mental stops. In other words, they keep the stop in their heads and have the discipline to sell if the stop is reached. However, they still know in advance what has to happen in the market to prove that their original buy decision was wrong.

> There will *always* be another stock to buy.

One problem with stops is that the market can drop sharply to hit your stop and then begin major rallies. Your original decision seemed good, but you had a loss on the trade. You are then tempted to ignore stops in the future, but that would be a grave mistake.

Why a mistake? Because it would force emotion back into the mix and you will hold on to a losing position because taking a loss is unpleasant. You will hope that the market will make you whole by allowing you to 'get out even'. That is one of the more dangerous goals in the financial world. Rational analysis is set aside in favour of prayer.

You may get stopped out and miss a big move but you will never get caught with a big loss. There will always be another stock to buy. Say that aloud right now, even if you are not alone. There will *always* be another stock to buy.

Would you buy it right now, at its current price?

In a perfect world, a computer could monitor hundreds of variables, from interest rates to politics, to constantly reevaluate your portfolio. In the real world, you can simply ask yourself periodically 'Would I buy this stock now?' Here are some questions with which to start:

■ My price objective has been reached. Would I buy it again at this price?

■ My price objective has not yet been reached. Would I buy it here even though I missed the first few points?

■ The market has stalled. Is my stock still looking good on its own?

■ News has come out. Did my stock react properly to it?

There are many reasons to sell a stock or a market. Most of them can be distilled down to the technical condition of the stock itself. Others come from the outside world. For our purposes, there are three important points:

■ Are you satisfied with the profit you have made already?

■ Has the stock or market simply stopped rising?

■ Has the price rise changed the risk/reward ratio to an unfavourable state?

These questions provide a good framework for the decision and they are not all that complicated to ask and to answer.

21 A word about your ego

An ego is a terrible thing to have. It forces you to depend on the market to bail you out of a wrong decision. Have you ever said to yourself 'I don't want to take a loss so I'll sell when I get back to even'? How many times do you actually get that chance?

> *'I'd rather be right than President'* – Senator Barry Goldwater, during an unsuccessful election run for US President.

Remember why you are investing.

Well, the Senator never got to be President. If you carry that attitude, you may be morally superior to your competitors, but they will end up with more money. Remember why you are investing.

Here is your new mantra. 'I'd rather make money than make a good market call.'

You will be wrong and probably a lot more than you would care to be. The secret is to deal with that properly. If you are wrong, admit it early. The market will not bail you out. Your bank account does not care how smart you are or if you embarrassed yourself in front of your investment club.

With all due respects to the late Senator Goldwater, he would not have made a good technical investor. The bottom line is to be President, i.e. profitable.

An ego? Leave it at the door.

part

5

Tools and case studies

What do you really need to get started?

In today's computerized, networked and instant world, the trading advantages go to those who make the best use of the best technology. Yet, the markets themselves are the same under their flashy surfaces as they were hundreds of years ago. Those with assets make deals with those who do not have them. Supply and demand still rule. While the sheer size and scope of the markets has become more than a person can monitor and analyze by hand, we can still apply the same concepts to them with basic technology. Do we need four computer screens, live data, a spreadsheet model and streaming news? The professionals might. You do not. You are not doing this full time. You are not even relying on technical analysis as your sole method of decision making. This chapter will look at a few of the components the professionals use and see if they are right for you.

> Supply and demand still rule.

Real-time data

Real-time simply means you see trades, bids and offers within seconds of their occurrences. You are viewing the markets at virtually the same time as those who make them. In contrast, end-of-day data shows market summaries (open, high, low and close). The bulk of analysis done by investors works fine with this data.

Live stock quotes scrolling across the bottom of your television screen are always impressive. Ask yourself if you can read those letters and numbers as fast as they are offered. Do you even know what stock the symbols are representing? Scrolling market quotes are pure entertainment and cannot help you invest.

What about quoting services that can deliver live prices to your home computer or your personal pager (beeper)? This is much more of a tool because you decide what information will display. Again, do you need this to invest? Unless you are employing a trading strategy where that last ⅛ point is the critical trigger to your plan, this sort of information is still more style than substance.

Real-time data is good if you are a short-term trader. Perhaps you are sophisticated enough to build market indicators on trade data to be used on longer-term investments. Keeping in mind your goal of supplementing your own analysis, real-time data is not necessary for analysis. It is good, however, to keep track of your target stocks or current portfolio to see if they have reached your predetermined buy or sell points during the trading day.

Bonus points for you if your data vendor offers earnings, dividends and other fundamental data history for charting.

Charting software

Without charting software, you will have to pour through the financial tables in your local newspaper to find each day's data and then plot them by hand. How many stocks can you follow in that way? The answer is probably not too many. Even though you do not need real-time data, you do need to be able to track hundreds, if not thousands, of different stocks over the course of your investing career. You will not have to track them all at the same time but you can watch several dozen at any one time.

There are many good, basic charting programs available to meet this need. Unfortunately, most of them will force you, as a non-full-time professional, to manage the data your system collects. The high-end packages often come complete with the data feed and can offer central database maintenance services as part of the package. If you plan to be a portfolio manager, this would be indispensable. If you are managing your own small group of stocks, this becomes an unnecessary luxury.

As charting software gets more sophisticated, the database management function is sure to get easier. Many services already come with single-button data refreshes and can even go out to the Internet to automatically find any data you may be missing. Since thousands of professional and semi-professional traders working in home offices use these services today, database maintenance cannot be too complex.

So what kind of software do you need? As you can tell from this book, a casual investor or investment club needs only the basics. This type of technician is not scanning the world's markets for the best opportunities.

Rather, he or she wants to reinforce decision making by making sure any current or proposed holdings have supporting technical conditions. They also want to know when the charts turn negative, prompting further research for the right time to sell.

What your charting package must have

In order to analyze the world's markets, your software must be able to draw certain type of price charts, a few studies and trendlines and be flexible to display the data in several views and time frames.

Price charts

Bar charts are a must. Bars display open, high, low and close prices for each day, and are the basic units of western technical analysis. Candle charts use the same data and most charting software can draw both.

Line charts: These charts connect close prices in a continuous plot. They are very valuable to get a feel for the trend without cluttering the screen with too much data.

Flexible time frames: You need to view the data in daily and weekly format. Daily charts summarize the trading for a single day. Weekly charts do the same for a calendar week.

Charts with intraday time frames, such as five-minute and hourly charts, will not be available if the data feed does not support this type of data. It is not available in non-real-time feeds. If you require live quotes, then your data feed can supply trade-by-trade information to build intraday charts but again, you really do not need them at this stage.

Studies

Volume must be available for each day. For items that do not report volume, such as market indices and currencies, there needs to be a substitute. These include underlying volume (the sum of the 30 stocks in the Dow-Jones Industrial Average) and trade count (the number of transactions each day). The number of trades per day can substitute for actual traded volume in most cases.

Momentum readings. Any of the more popular momentum studies will work. Most packages come with the RSI, Stochastics, MACD and a host of others.

Moving averages are standard fare for charting software. Be sure that you can adjust the number of days or weeks used in the averages and that you are not limited to some small parameter. 200-day averages are a must.

One element of charting that comes from the data feed instead of the software is the *breadth indicator* group. Advance-decline, number of net new highs and others are usually broadcast by the data feed vendor and then charted by the software.

Tools

Drawing tools are very important to allow you to impose some order on what seems like a chaotic chart. Trendlines can define the slope of a rally or decline. They can also be combined to draw triangles and other technical patterns. Retracement lines allow you to find hidden support and resistance without measuring by hand.

If you will be faxing any charts to your own clients or making presentations to your investment club, then you will appreciate the ability to write text comments on the charts before you print them.

Measuring tools allow you to find implied price targets and market cycles as well as allowing you to draw clear markings on any chart you wish to present to your co-investors. The software should have some way to divide a vertical distance (price) you highlight with $\frac{1}{3}$, $\frac{1}{2}$ and $\frac{2}{3}$ retracement levels. Even better would be a cycle-finder tool that allows you to measure a horizontal distance (time) and replicate it across the chart.

Mathematics. 1+1=2

The heading for this paragraph sums up your need for complex mathematical modelling, spreadsheets and complex calculations. Your analysis will not be based on quantitative analysis so leave that to the professional in a large organization. The professional is looking for a small profit per share on huge positions. You are looking for a large profit on small positions and do not have to worry about that degree of precision.

Internet

The Internet has everything mentioned above, including real-time and intraday charting with formulas. It can be a good source for the beginner technician since most information is free. Keep in mind that providers of free services are not obliged to provide you with a complete service of what you need when you need it. Data may not be reliable, either.

Do not be afraid to use it. Just remember what it is and, more importantly, what it is not.

Your child's geometry tools

Away from the computer screen, if you plan to present your findings to a group or review your portfolio on your commuter train on your way to your day job, keep a small plastic *ruler* in your briefcase. You can draw trendlines and chart patterns quickly, although maybe not as precisely, as your software.

A *compass* will allow you to measure patterns and project targets for possible breakouts. It will allow you to compare chart features to one another in terms of both price (vertical height) and time (horizontal length). You will be able to measure turning points in the market to find cycles, as well.

Do not be shy. If you are careful, you can even use the compass on your computer screen to do the measuring. It is probably still faster than the built-in tools.

23 Building your technical toolbox

OK, so now you have grasped the concepts of technical analysis and can put several to use in making your investment decisions. The next step is to balance your approach to analysis with the proper tools.

Like quality carpentry, quality technical analysis requires the right tool for the right job. While a hand saw can cut wood to build a table, a power saw with

> Quality technical analysis requires the right tool for the right job.

built-in guides can do it with a much higher degree of precision. Conversely, the back end of a screwdriver can pound a nail but choosing the right tool, a hammer, protects both the carpenter and the tool. This chapter will outline what tools should be in a good technical toolbox.

Technical tasks

Technical tasks are simply the analyses in the four main areas that technicians consider. These are *price, volume, time* and *sentiment*. Many of today's widely-used indicators focus on only one of these areas. Further, many of today's technicians use only a few indicators, leaving out one or more sectors of analysis completely. This is like building a table with two or three legs. It may stand up for a while but it will not be solid enough to deal with shifting or heavy loads.

Since the goal of any market analysis is to buy and sell an asset to make money in the differential between price paid and price received, *price* is necessarily the most important factor. It is not a surprise that most market analysis revolves around this element. Price patterns, such as triangles and gaps, are used extensively. Measures of price momentum, such as the RSI and rate of change are popular. Methods of smoothing out market noise, such as exponential moving average systems, are created all the time.

Volume is the next area and is important in gauging public participation in any market move. Liquidity, open interest and breadth are all terms used here. Liquidity measures how easy it will be to trade (turnover) and how much catalyst is needed to cause a price change. The more liquidity, the easier it will be to get a competitive price and the easier it will be to buy and sell large amounts of stock.

Open interest, while usually confined to the futures markets, measures how many participants have put their money on the line by establishing either long or short positions. 'Shares outstanding' in the stock market is not quite the same but it does indicate how much stock is available (short sales excluded). Available stock is the potential supply that can be offered for trading.

Breadth covers such areas as how various market sectors participating in any price moves and how much money is flowing into or out of the market.

The next area of analysis is *time*. Accumulation, distribution, bull phases and bear phases are common to all markets and each stage takes a certain amount of time to complete. Together they form the market cycle and knowing where you are in the cycle helps in making the investment decision. Further, the relative lengths of each cycle component and their durations yield clues to market direction. Seasonal analysis began with agricultural commodities as they progressed through their growing, harvesting and selling seasons but can be seen in all markets. Economic and political cycles affect the financial markets as capital flows and productivity change.

The least understood area of analysis is *sentiment* analysis. This covers such areas as degree of speculation, public opinion and consensus. It is measured by relative activities in speculative instruments, such as options, and polls of bullish opinions. Both rely on the 'burning match' theory in which the flame is passed from investor to investor until there is nobody left to take the match. The last one holding it gets burned. In the markets, as bullish opinion spreads, eventually everyone will have bought so there will be nobody left to whom the last investors can sell. No demand means the end of the rally. This can also be measured subjectively in the media as glowing bullish news is reported only when the newspaper buyer and TV viewer are ready to receive it. Again, when the public has an overall bullish consensus, there is nobody left to buy.

You should be three-deep at every position. Professor Henry Pruden, Golden Gate University, referring to three indicators from each of the four analytical areas.

Tools for each technical task

The most common tools in each area are outlined in Figure 23.1. Unless noted otherwise, these have already been covered. Sentiment indicators have not been covered in depth.

Price	Trend identification	■ Trendlines, channels Smoothing, moving averages
	Patterns	■ Triangles, rectangles, flags, gaps ■ Candlesticks (in Chapter 7)
	Momentum	■ Momentum indicators such as the relative strength index, departure, Stochastics, MACD ■ Bollinger bands (in Chapter 7)
	Relative levels	■ Benchmarking, relative strength to market ■ Log scaling
Volume	Participation	■ Volume, cumulative volume
	Liquidity	■ Market capitalization, turnover (both of these can help measure how much stock is out there)
	Breadth	■ Up-down volume ■ Advance-decline ■ Sector analysis
Time	Cycles (in Chapter 7)	■ Form (translation) ■ Seasonal ■ Economic, political
	Time frame	■ Short, medium, long ■ Cyclical (minor swing) vs Secular (major trend)
	Extent	■ Length of trend or base ■ Relation of correction to trend
Sentiment	Speculation (excesses)	■ Options activity, put-call ratio ■ Junk bonds, initial public offerings ■ Margin levels, mutual fund cash levels ■ Commitment of traders report ■ Effects of good and bad news
	Consensus	■ Percent of newsletters bullish or bearish ■ Public opinion
	Anecdotal	■ Magazine covers ■ Hem lines, Superbowl

Fig 23.1 ■ Technical tools

Combination tools

No beginner's book on any subject would be complete without exposing the reader to some of the more advanced concepts of the subject. In technical analysis, some indicators are designed to cover more than one analysis area. Most of them require the user to have a complete comfort, if not fluency, in the tenets of technical analysis so the following table is presented more as an advertisement for advanced learning.

Price and time	■ Market profile (shows time spent at each price during the day, forms a value area on the chart)
	■ MESA (maximum entropy spectral analysis, finds cycles in the data and projects them forward)
Price and volume	■ Money flow (price times volume summed per trade, used as a supply/demand indicator)
	■ Equivolume (bars have width in proportion to volume, used to allocate significance to price bars)
Price and sentiment	■ Elliott waves (wave structure follows public emotions, can identify ebb and flow of trading activity – covered briefly in Chapter 7)

Fig 23.2 ■ Combination tools

There are many variations of each study available but there is a limit to how much data one can reasonably combine into a trading strategy. Mechanical systems and artificial intelligence can go beyond this limit but in return for better analysis, they require greater expertise, computer power and discipline to set up and use. While the latest gadgets may be available to the carpenter, most practitioners will do fine work with a basic set of tools. As long as each is matched to the job at hand, the resulting quality is limited only by the skill of the craftsman.

Final advice

Before unleashing a new crop of eager, but unseasoned, novice technicians on the markets, there are a few pearls of wisdom to be handed down:

- *Let the market talk to you.* If you cannot determine if it is saying up, down or sideways using simple tools and unambiguous interpretation, then find another stock to analyze. If you force your analysis you will, in effect, be telling the market what to do. The market is the boss, not you.

- *Be flexible.* Follow the 'spirit of the law' rather than the 'letter of the law'. In other words do not be so strict with your rules that you miss the trend. Set trendlines and patterns loosely so that they can describe what is really happening in the market. Strict construction may be right according to the textbook but may produce unusable results.

- *Do not chase a stock.* The last ⅛ is never worth it. There is *always* another opportunity.

- *Leave your ego at the door.* If you are wrong, admit it immediately. You may miss an occasional star performer but you will never be saddled with a major loser. Remember, you would rather make money than be right.

- *Getting out even is a losing strategy.* Never, never, never think that you should wait to sell a loser when you can get even. If you buy at a price of 55 and it goes down 5 points, it would have to rally 10 per cent to get you out even. Does that seem possible in light of your conclusion that you think it was a bad purchase? Sell your losers immediately after you decide you were wrong to buy them in the first place.

- *Does your analysis make sense?* Have you weighed risk against reward? Are your chart patterns commensurate with the previous trend? Remember, a 12-month rally of 50 per cent cannot be corrected by a 2-week, 2 per cent flag.

Good luck to you. Start out slowly and build on your new knowledge. As you get more comfortable, add more indicators to give you the big picture. When you can do that, you may be tempted to rely solely on technical analysis. You will be in good company.

CASE STUDY
The perfect world

Now that you know what charting and technical analysis are all about and that they are not going to replace your current means of stock selection at this time, the pieces can be assembled together in a case study. This involves the major areas of recognizing trends, finding patterns and using supporting studies to assess the stock market and pick a winning stock.

Here's the process:

- Determine if conditions are favourable for equity assets using our current analytical techniques (earnings, inflation, etc …)
- If they are fair to good, then determine what sectors of the market would be best to focus upon.
- Now that the best sectors are found, which stocks should you buy?
- What technical tools should you apply to help?
- What is the upside target likely to be?
- What will cause you to change your mind and get out soon after buying?
- What will cause you to sell the stock early, before it reaches its upside target?
- Do you have to sell when the stock reaches its target?

You may not cover them all individually, but this is the thinking going on behind the scenes.

Are conditions favourable to equity assets?

We're not going to assess whether investing in stocks is better than real estate or bonds or thoroughbred racehorses. That is more fundamental at this stage. Advanced technicians can do that purely through technical analysis by exploiting whatever relationships may exist between stocks, bonds, currencies, commodities and other economic indices, but that is beyond the scope of this book. Let's just say that the decision has been made to invest or trade stocks already so the goal is to pick the best ones.

As stated earlier, the stock market is really a market for stocks and only the strongest of bull or bear markets will move stock selection to the side. That said, why do you need to analyze the market as a whole? The answer is in the boat analogy again. A rising tide will lift all boats, unless there is something seriously wrong with the individual boat. A falling tide will drop them all with the exception of the unusual boat possessing some special features. In market terms, that means fundamental news or developments, such as new contracts, new breakthroughs or new financial deals will move some stocks higher in bear markets.

The risk here is to determine whether to pick stocks that are unusual or are simply going to outperform the rising market to make you the most money. A pure technical analyst will need only the chart and supporting data for the individual stocks to determine whether to buy or sell. Knowing the conditions for stocks in general can only enhance the analysis, not make it possible. After all, a good chart says buy whether the market is rising, falling or staying put. Remember the twist to the analogy, the rising tide raises most boats. It is that word 'most' that makes stock selection important at all times for *maximum* profit. An ordinary stock rising with the market will give you an ordinary profit, not the maximum possible profit at that given time.

Let's assume your other analysis says that stocks should be a part of your total investment portfolio. Here is how to tackle the problem from a purely technical standpoint. In a few paragraphs, we'll translate that into the real world where you have a few leads, your fundamental research has pointed you to a few industries and your broker has made his recommendations. Your selection within that subset can be dramatically improved using technical analysis.

Studies have shown that sector analysis, the analysis of business areas within the stock market, can yield superior stock selection. Rather than back that claim up with specific studies and profits, let's look at it logically. First, you must agree that there is a business cycle in the economy. As the economy grows, certain supplies are needed from energy to capital goods to the money needed to finance growth. Consumers alter their habits in purchasing necessities and luxury items. Resources become depleted and labour needs change. There, in a nutshell, we have covered the economy from start to maturity to decline. Let's turn this jargon into types of companies just to see how investing in different industries can return different profits in different parts of the cycle. Again, we are only talking of sectors and industries right now, not whether Coke or Pepsi is the better soft drink company to buy. For now, we only care whether soft drink and other beverage makers are good to own in general.

- Energy sector – This includes such companies as Elf Aquatine, Royal Dutch and Schlumberger.

- Industrial and Capital Goods – Think of the companies that will sell to an expanding economy such as Navistar and Cisco.

- Financial – If businesses are expanding, then they need to finance operations. Try Mitsubishi and Citigroup.

- Consumer Necessities – People always need to feed and clothe themselves. They also have stable demand for such items as ethical drugs, cigarettes and alcoholic beverages. What does it say about the economy when these stocks rise faster than the stocks associated with prosperity and risk-taking?

- Consumer Luxuries/Cyclicals – When things are starting to go well throughout the economy, people will spend more on non-essential items such as Rolls Royce cars, Rolex watches and even new housing. Who makes them? Who supplies to the companies that make them? The term 'cyclicals' also applies to capital goods, as strong companies tend to invest in their futures.

- Resources – Who controls the commodities? This sector tends to bring up the rear in a bull market by taking leadership near its end. Supplies tighten and inflation is likely to be picking up in a mature economy so hard asset mining, growing and owning companies do best.

To sum up, if the economy is down and inflation is high, some sectors will still make money. If things are good, other sectors will be better to maximize profits.

No matter what the condition of the stock markets, global economies, interest rates and inflation, some stocks will go up and some will go down. This is clearly evidenced in the lists of stocks making new 52-week highs and lows in the daily business paper. Even during the great bull market of the 1990s many stocks were either left behind or fell to pieces. After all, if a company goes bankrupt, the condition of the market is irrelevant.

Where should a pure technician start? The answer is in the business cycle. How can you determine where you are in the cycle using technical analysis? This answer is relative strength. Which sectors are starting to rise faster or even fall slower than the general market? Are gold stocks rising faster? Chances are you are nearer to the end and the decline in the cycle rather than at the beginning, or rise. Go with it. Sure, a select few stocks will do well when they theoretically should not, but you are trying to maximize profits, not nail down every winning stock out there. The stocks with the best odds for success will come from the sectors that the business cycle is favouring.

Keep in mind that you are not trying to time the entire market. You are just trying to find the best places to put the money you have already allocated to stocks. You can leave that exercise to others.

Again, this book is not about converting you to the technical, side in lieu of the fundamentals. Let's see how you can meld these two disciplines into a strategy that works no matter what the markets are doing.

What sectors of the market are good?

Choosing the best sectors can be done through a simple ratio chart. We have called this relative strength analysis because what we will do is measure each sector relative to the market. Is the relationship between technology stocks and the broad market index improving or deteriorating? In other words, is the ratio going up or down?

If you utilize the various sector or industry indices available in most major stock markets around the world you will be able to run this ratio for each country. As the world becomes more connected, watch to see when pan-continental and pan-world sector indices arise. Don't worry about this. Someone in some brokerage or news company will put them together for you so you will forever use their company's name in your work. Who do you think invented the Dow Jones Industrial Average or the FTSE 100?

Simply take the ratios of each sector to the relevant market index (S&P 500, TOPIX, DAX, Hang Seng, you name it) over your desired time frame. In other words, is the ratio rising or falling over the past month, six-months or five years. The longer your investment time frame, the longer your comparisons should be. Rank your ratios to find the strongest and weakest. Finally, chart the ratios and apply trendlines. We did this on page 140 to see when the car industry was starting to lag the US stock market.

The strongest ratios mean the strongest groups and as long as the trendlines holding up the chart of those ratios remain intact, they represent the best places to begin your stock selection.

What stocks within the good sectors are the best to buy?

Now, let's turn to our recommended list, fundamental selections and other members of our 'hot list'. Do they come from the strongest groups? If not, they may still be good but they will require exceptionally strong technical opinions to make them buck the conditions prevailing in their sectors and industry groups.

Let's say some of the hot list stocks come from the strongest sectors. We now turn to the charts to find positive trends, positive pattern breakouts and supporting data such as volume, momentum and sentiment. Rather than rehash previous examples here, the reader is invited to look back at the sections on these topics for review.

Risk assessment

Even stocks with good charts may still not be the best candidates to purchase. Does the chart suggest the risk will be worth the potential reward? Here, you measure the upside target or strength of the trend and compare that profit to the potential loss if you are wrong (stopped out). A good rule to follow is that the reward must be greater than or equal to three times the risk. In other words, risking 3 points of loss on a stock that has an upside profit potential of only 5 points is not prudent risk management. Think of the racetrack where the longshot horse has a payoff of 10 to 1 or more. The favourite has better odds to win and therefore the payout is much less in the 3 to 2 area. What happens when the longshot moves to 50 to 1 odds? That risk/reward equation might make taking that bet worth the risk.

An important factor in investment success is knowing when to sell. There are two reasons to sell: either if it was wrong to buy in the first place or the stock has reached its full potential as indicated by your analysis. Sometimes, you need to sell when we were right but market conditions have changed before our target was reached. Think about what has to happen in order to make you sell. Do this in advance and you will sleep well at night.

How do you set the 'I was wrong' level? Usually, if the stock ignores the signal that got you to buy in the first place, it is time to admit defeat. This could mean falling below the breakout level from a chart pattern such as a triangle, reversing course immediately after breaking above horizontal resistance or just not rallying when the chart says it should.

Selling at your target price is easy. All you have to do is be sure the chart is not screaming for you to buy more at that price. The hardest sell will be before the target is actually reached. Here, you must be flexible enough to spot a change in the trend, momentum or sector strength when it happens and wise enough to leave your ego out of the decision. For example, if you buy a triangle breakout and the stock never sets a fresh new high. The triangle you were so sure about may have been an incorrect assessment leaving luck to give you a small profit. Knowing that the triangle was incorrect will allow you to reassess the position and steal away with a profit you may not deserve. Your astute mid-course correction earned you the right to keep it.

Pull the trigger

In a phrase, when you have completed your analysis and chosen your stocks, go buy them. Do not worry if they are perfect, as the market will tell you that soon enough. The adage in poker is 'know when to hold 'em and know when to fold 'em' and it applies to the stock market. You are going to have some losing trades so expect them and work to minimize their impact on your portfolio.

It all sounds good, right? However, all of this assumes a lot of readily available information and chart patterns that are clearly defined. In the next chapter, we will go over what really happens out there and how you can make the most of the imperfect information and conditions that really exist.

CASE STUDY
The real world

The perfect world is a nice place in which to live and invest but unfortunately, that is not the reality of the financial markets. There is a saying 'the market will try to do whatever it can to cause the most people to lose the most money'. Before beginning any financial exercise, remember that the market will rarely present itself clearly. This is the chapter where technical analysis can really be used to determine if your stocks are good or if your broker is recommending winners.

> In the real world, nothing follows the theories.

In the real world, nothing follows the theories we learn in school. Hospital patients do not respond equally to the same medicines. Economies do not respond to stimuli in the same way each time. Stocks do not follow technical patterns to break out with the same power or even the same direction.

It is nice to know if financial assets are in favour but what if they are not? You still need to do something with your investment capital. The overall climate for financial assets and specifically for stocks, bonds and cash will determine your asset mix. The climate itself can turn very quickly so you cannot act with certainty.

The best you can do is determine two things. The first is, how aggressive should you be? No matter what the climate is, certain gains are to be made in stocks and bonds. Maybe you will have to temper your expectations on the rate of return you can achieve but the goal is the same. This sounds a lot like a lot of hard work, but you already do this now with your current form of analysis.

Second, you must determine the proper sectors of the market on which to focus. If returns from industrial and service company stocks are poor, then you should stay with key industries that people need in good times and in bad. They may not be flashy but that is not why you are investing. If it is, then you should take a closer look at day trading futures and options. Is inflation very high? If so, certain financial sectors will not be good investments but perhaps sectors that own commodities would be better.

Once you decide on how aggressive to be and in what sectors to look, the application of the technical tools is the same. A trendline break will be just as meaningful.

Examine a few charts of stocks and indices from several sectors. You can assume that they were recommended to you by either your brokers or your own top-down analysis using the perfect world characteristics outlined above and in Chapter 25. However, once you have your list of potential candidates, how you got to them becomes irrelevant. The technical chart will stand on its own to guide you to a trading decision. After you look at some 'big picture' types of charts and follow a few through their non-textbook travels, you will look at a few purchase candidates to compare, the goal being to select the best one to buy.

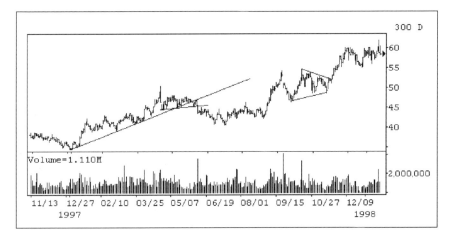

Fig 26.1 ■ Delta Airlines

Figure 26.1 is a daily chart of Delta Airlines for 300 days from November 1996 through to January 1998. With this amount of data, the bars become a bit compressed but that is fine for these purposes. As can be seen, there was a rising trend in early 1997. In April, the stock peaked and made a sharp reversal lower. Was this an important sell signal? In retrospect, it was not. Shorter-term charts would have showed an overbought condition where buyers got ahead of themselves by bidding up prices too aggressively. There was nothing special about the volume chart shown below the prices so you probably would have taken a step back to see how things developed.

Over the next few weeks, the market moved sideways. A small bounce off the rising trendline would have made you more confident that the trend was still intact but soon thereafter, prices slipped below the line. Now what do you do? The textbook would say to sell. After all, the stock stopped going up and then broke its supporting trendline.

After only two days, prices stopped falling at what turned out to be the bottom border of a triangle pattern. Did you know that it was a triangle pattern before the bounce? It was not clear but it was there. The textbook leads you to believe that the triangle support and trendline support should meet at the breakdown point because if either were broken, you would sell. The trendline was broken, but the stock did not keep going down. When the triangle was broken, there were two indications that the trend had changed from bullish to bearish and the increase in volume on the second breakdown day confirms it.

Rewind for a moment. Would you really have known about that triangle? Again, it was there early, but in the heat of the investment decision, it most likely would not have been noticeable. Without seeing it, you had to rely on the trendline break. Since the trendline was a relatively strong technical pattern due to seven to nine market touches, depending on the strictness of the rules applied, you would still have made the correct decision. The addition of the triangle adds confidence to act before it becomes too late.

Now, you are probably saying to yourself, 'I'm a long-term investor'. To that, technical analysis says that the chart could have easily been 300 weeks, not days, long. The analysis would have been the same.

Now move along in time to the triangle pattern of October 1997. At that time, the US stock market was recovering from the Asian market debacle and the resultant effect on the technology sector. Delta is not a technology stock. After the excitement abated and investors were looking once again at the technical and fundamental underpinnings of the market, the focus turned to the steady decline in energy prices. Crude oil and its related products were caught in a strong bear market. When this happens, all market watchers look for sectors that benefit from this condition and, of course, one of the biggest energy users is the airline sector.

The triangle in Delta suggested that the stock was on hold as investors decided if the low energy market would offset the possible economic affects of the Asian problems. When the stock broke out higher from the triangle, it was telling you that the low energy prices had won and it was time to buy. Naturally, you did not get the textbook confirmation of an expansion in volume that would have given you confidence. The small rise was good enough and due to the measured height of the triangle, you anticipated a ten-point gain. The stock obliged in what was an unusually accurate move.

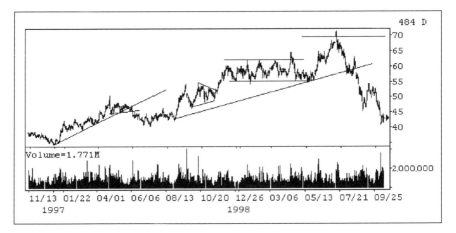

Fig 26.2 ■ Delta Airlines later

In Figure 26.2, another nine months of trading are added. After reaching its ten-point objective, Delta moved sideways for several months. The rectangle pattern was drawn but it did not contain prices well. You had to ignore the January false breakdown and were possibly faked out in the April false breakout to the upside. Perhaps a short-term oriented trader was taking advantage of this pattern by selling the tops and buying the bottoms. You as an investor were not very happy, since you got no clear buy or sell signals.

What you did not see then was the long-term rising trendline from January 1997. It is clear now that it is several months past the rectangle pattern but back then, it was of little help. Now move forward a bit further.

In June 1997, the rectangle had run sideways into the long-term trendline. Now, the line would have been seen. Knowing that when consolidation patterns run into larger trendlines the trendlines usually win, you start to look for reasons to buy. You know that a downside break here would be a very clear sell signal but until that happens, you have to assume that an upside move is more likely.

Based on the chart, you would have missed the run from the rectangle bottom to the top. Perhaps, if you were playing the rectangle by buying the bottom, you would have profited but, again, that is not a long-term investment strategy. The spike in volume when the stock moved off that floor might have triggered aggressive investors to jump in, but this is not in a classroom and the odds were not quite high enough for the average investor.

When prices reached the rectangle top, you begin to look for signs of an upside breakout. The stock stalled between the rectangle top and the false breakout peak of April. A tighter view of the market showed that the pattern emerging during the 'stall' was a bullish flag so when you got the upside break there, you had a good buy signal. The stock rallied another ten points, which was the height of the rectangle.

Extra credit: Look at the section of the chart from the false breakout to the flag. What other pattern do you see?

Answer: Cup with handle.

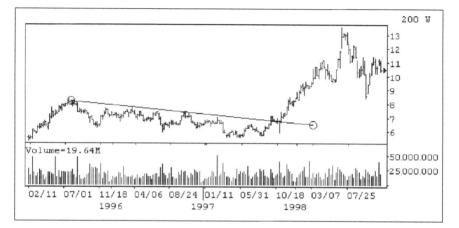

Fig 26.3 ■ News Corporation

If you are still not convinced that technical analysis can help the long-term investor, then this next example is for you.

News Corp. (Figure 26.3, four years of weekly data) ended a long slow decline in late 1997. Given the size, length and form of the pattern seen on the chart, the upside breakout was a very good buy signal. You can see a clear transition from a bear phase to a bull phase. Would you have found this stock on your own using technical screening software? Maybe a professional technician would have seen it based on the rising bottoms seen before the breakout. Perhaps a money flow indicator, not normally available to individual investors, would have shown an accumulation of shares and an increase in demand. Your brokerage firm's technical analysis research team, if it had one, probably would have that access.

> Your job is to ride the major part of the move.

More likely, your broker would have received a report from the firm's fundamental analyst saying that the prospects for the media sector had improved in the age of the Internet and that News Corp's businesses had begun to turn profits. The early profits have been missed but that should not bother you. Your job is to ride the major part of the move.

Take a closer look at the declining trendline. The big decision is where to draw it. As drawn above, the line hits three peaks very well. In October 1997, there is a small upside breakout but the stock fails to go anywhere. Even worse, it took a big, albeit short-lived, tumble with the Australian market as a whole in reaction to the Asian market situation. Rather than curse technical analysis for providing yet another ambiguous trading signal, you should take the opportunity to revise the trendline to capture this new data. While you may have suffered a blow to your ego due to the false breakout, you have set yourself up to be ready when the true breakout finally arrives. When it did, the market never looked back.

This looks great – in hindsight. Of course you can rationalize the revision of trendlines and ignore small temporary losses after the fact. The real fact is that the early false breakout was not a very high confidence event from the start. This author likes to see a convincing breakout in terms of price action, momentum, volume and/or group action. Consider this insider's tip No. 1. This stock poked its head above the trendline but never broke free from it. A half-day of trading in the absence of confirmation is not good enough. When the stock retraced back to the trendline the very next day, you should have taken the cue that this breakout was not very solid.

To rephrase that, a stock should break free from the trendline to give a high confidence signal that it really has broken out. Yes, you will lose some of the potential profit buy waiting, but weigh that against the risk of being wrong.

The subsequent action took place on the trendline itself in a flag-like pattern. Insider's tip No. 2, when a market hits a resistance and does not quickly fall away from it, it is a sign of strength. Even in this unusual case where there was a one-week shock, the quick recovery kept the bullish nature of the pattern alive.

Now you really have to reconcile a few discrepancies. In the Delta Airlines example (Figure 26.2), the market reached a support level at the bottom of that rectangle without quickly bouncing higher. This should have been bearish since it did not react properly to a support. In that case, the market was also in the vicinity of a longer-term trendline support and given the relative length of time spent before bouncing, the bearish assumption made after failing to rise off the rectangle support was overruled. Now revise insider's tip No. 2. If a market trends into a resistance and does not quickly fall away from it, it is a sign of strength. Easing into a resistance in a sideways manner should be taken less seriously as a bad sign.

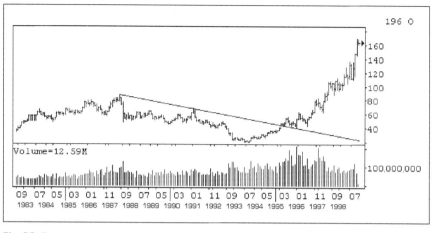

Fig 26.4 ■ IBM

Now go really long term. IBM shows the same transition from bearish to bullish that you saw in News Corporation in monthly format in Figure 26.3. As you can see, it took a decade for the stock to recover its 1987 pre-crash highs. Was the declining trendline very strong or even very obvious? Drawing it on the chart does provide a framework for analysis. The best signal might have been the break above resistance set by the 1991 interim peak. While this would have missed more than 20-points of profit, it was still good enough for the remaining 90–100 points. Again, you are trying to identify whether a stock is in a trending mode and then jump on it for the majority of the ride.

Deutsche Bank traded in a range from mid 1994 to early 1997 before finally breaking out to the upside. This created a large base from which to launch a significant rally and prices quickly climbed to their upside target in only a few months. The target was derived by projecting the height of the range up from the breakout point and is highlighted in Figure 26.5. The length and height of the base for stocks, just as for the foundation of a building, determine how high prices can go.

If you could bolster your new knowledge by experience, you would be close to thinking like the pros. Figure 26.6 shows the Sterling/US dollar exchange rate for the time period leading up to the debacle of 1992. You did not have to be George Soros to get out before the carnage. This market was at resistance, broke a trendline on an outside-week reversal and sported a bearish RSI divergence. Further, it had failed to break above a resistance level so you can invoke insider's tip No. 2. You may not have become a billionaire like George but you could have adjusted your portfolio away from stocks that this sort of wild currency swing would have hurt.

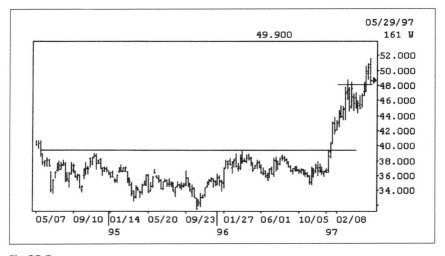

Fig 26.5 ■ **Deutsche Bank**

You have been concentrating on only a few of the many aspects of chart reading. The reason for this is that in most cases, they will provide enough insight into the status of the trend and the type of consolidation going on within patterns. Remember, markets move up, down or sideways. It sounds trite but that is all there can be when the only dependent variable is price and the only independent variable is time. Time itself is very simple since it can only move in one direction.

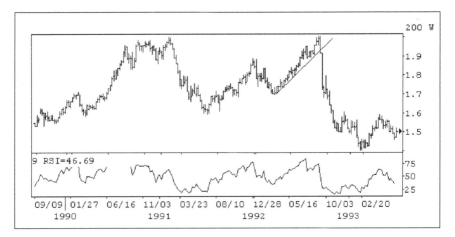

Fig 26.6 ■ **Sterling/US dollars**

With this in mind, consider some more examples.

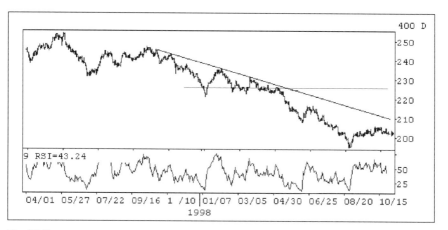

Fig 26.7 ■ CRB

Here is a great example of how a triangle and a trendline work together. Figure 26.7 shows 400 days of the Bridge/CRB index of commodities futures prices. Futures prices? Even though futures trading is something most will never do, you can still learn from this analysis. First, for the curious, the index was developed by the Commodities Research Bureau decades ago as a way to measure the broad levels of commodity prices. Its most common use is as an inflation gauge, although many would say it is a better indicator for the bond market. As a stock market investor, you can use it to measure the health of the commodity asset class and compare it to financial assets (interest rates, economic growth) and to cash.

From Figure 26.7 you can see immediately that the trend had been down as commodity prices had been falling for nearly two years. The first question you should be asking is 'Why the trendline drawn from the highest peak seen?' The answer can be found earlier in this book in Chapter 6. Simply put, the line drawn from the peak would only touch the market twice and be a poor representation of what is actually occurring. The line drawn from the second peak is better because it touches the market seven times early on and comes much closer to the late rally off the August 1998 bottom. Again, for your purposes, strict construction of trendlines and other features may be more accurate but yield fewer usable clues as to market direction. You are not trying to be 'right'. You are trying to make money.

For the first half of 1998, the index made lower highs but failed to make lower lows. The lows it did make were actually progressively higher so you conclude that the market has lost its short-term trend in favour of a sideways move. However, all of this took place beneath the longer-term declining trendline so the major trend remained down.

During the first bottom of the triangle in January, you did not know that there was such a strong trendline developing. All you had at that time was the oversold reading in various momentum indicators such as the relative strength index pictured in Figure 26.7. When the index made its first peak within the triangle, you still did not know about the trendline but again, the momentum of the market had reached an extreme, telling you it might not be a good time to jump in and buy.

Once the index fell from that peak, you were finally able to draw the trendline on the chart. From there, you could watch the triangle develop fully into a usable pattern and when it was broken to the downside in May, you could have been reasonably confident that commodity prices were once again heading lower. You could even apply the measuring technique already outlined to predict the June low (first multiple of the pattern height projected down from the break) as well as the August low (second integral multiple) once the first level fell.

Fig 26.8 ■ PHLX Semiconductor Index

At times, some of the textbook patterns come to life in the real world just as you hope they would. A well-defined descending triangle breaks its support and the market plummets. Even better, that triangle breaks at the same time as a supporting trendline. This was the situation seen in the semiconductor sector in the US stock market in the third quarter of 1997.

In Figure 26.8, the rally in the Philadelphia stock exchange semiconductor index had stalled in mid-1997. As bulls and bears repositioned themselves, the swings in the market began to lessen. This showed growing uncertainty. Back in Chapter 8 you learned that triangles are usually signs that the market is resting before the next move in the same direction it was going before the pattern emerged. However, you also found out that the most important part about trading with triangles and other patterns is waiting for the market to actually break through the pattern boundaries before acting. In this case, the supposed bullish continuation pattern turned into a bearish reversal.

What happened there? Actually, nothing that you would not expect. While you might have been ready to buy the upside breakout, if you were really following the rules you would not have been fooled. You would have waited for the break.

Were there any clues that this triangle was a reversal? The declining top and flat bottom made it a descending triangle and hinted that something more than just a pause in the rally was at hand. Remember, patterns are formed when the actions of the bulls and the bears become more or less aggressive, respectively. Here, the bears were not waiting for higher prices to sell (on each successive peak within the triangle). The bulls, however, did wait for the same low price to be reached before buying and that tipped the supply–demand balance in favour of the bears.

In earlier examples, we mentioned that the late 1997 drop in major stock markets was related to the market collapses in Asia. Economists said that exports to Asia would drop dramatically and that technology stocks would fare the worst. The semiconductor index confirms that theory but notice when the index itself actually broke down. It was in early October. The 1997 global stock market panic occurred later that month. Technical analysis caught this development well before the economists and the news media.

The declining trend that followed the initial drop looks very clear on the chart shown. Again, you had no way of drawing that declining trendline until April 1998 so it did not do you much good back then. Other technical techniques would have to be employed and this takes you away from the basic focus of this book. So how did you know when to get back into this sector and feel better when your brokers started to suggest technology as the wave of the future? The declining trend was helpful but not really confidence inspiring. What should jump out of the chart at this point in your technical career is the 'W' pattern in August–October 1998. It can be subjectively called a double bottom pattern but the two bottoms are not exactly equal. Keeping an open mind you see that although the shape is not pure, it did have the other characteristics of a viable basing pattern and possible reversal.

First, the shape is clearly a 'W'. The market fell sharply, made a clear, yet temporary, recovery and fell back to its old low levels. The momentum study shown in Figure 26.8, the RSI, failed to return to its earlier low level when prices fell back to their old low and this set up a bullish divergence between the index and its indicator. (Prices actually fell below the old low so the divergence was even more meaningful.)

Great, the market made a nice pattern and had a divergence. What do you do about it and when? Again, refer back to Chapter 9 to see that the time to start nibbling at the market was when the index rose above the centre peak of the 'W'. At that point, the bear market had to be over because it had made a higher high and broke above a small resistance level. Remember that the definition of a bearish trend is a series of successive lower highs and lower lows. Here, there is a higher high. Add all the other technical signals and you end up with a positive reading on the semiconductor sector.

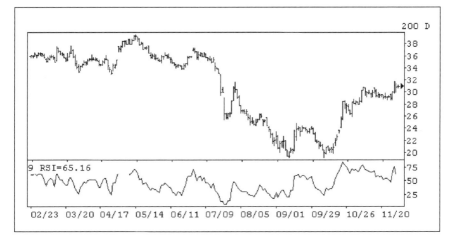

Fig 26.9 ■ St Jude Medical

Just to keep your head out of the perfect world, the chart of St. Jude Medical in Figure 26.9 illustrates the more common occurrence of the 'W' double bottom. The span of data is only 200 days so the 'W' appears to be wider than that of the semiconductor index but it is similar in both size and duration. What you need to learn here is that the bullish divergence condition appears at the wrong place. If this is true than it becomes a bad indicator but you can be flexible enough to spot the same meaning in the ambiguous patterns seen in this stock. Again, you see support at the 'W' bottom and a buy signal when the central peak is breached.

Summary

The charts will tell you what the market is doing and give signals as to what it will do next. The secret is not to anticipate the market but be prepared to act when the market tells you it is ready to go. Even real

> Be prepared to act when the market tells you it is ready to go.

world ambiguous patterns can be read like textbook examples if you relax some restrictions. As long as the spirit of the rules is not violated, they should still be powerful enough to give you the correct signals.

How good is your broker's stock?

When your broker tells you about a stock that is supposed to be good, start with the chart. You will need to answer these questions:

- What is the current trend and chart pattern?

- How have people been buying and selling it? (volume, momentum)

- If it is not trending, are there any positive imbalances to watch?

- What industry is it in and how is the group doing?

- How does it compare to other stocks?

When your broker's recommendation looks like nothing special

Sometimes the fundamental news is early. If your broker presents a stock that looks mediocre on the charts, watch it for several weeks. Sometimes technical analysis will signal when the time is finally right to buy.

> If your broker presents a stock that looks mediocre on the charts, watch it for several weeks.

Figure 27.1 shows the stock of Western Atlas which looked weak in early 1997. It gapped higher in May on a clear volume spike to break the consolidation zone and kick off a five-month rally. Gaps alone are important signals and combined with high volume these become very reliable. Fundamental reports do not change much from month to month. The fundamental buy signal could have happened before, during or after the price breakout. Technical analysis only signals at the breakout.

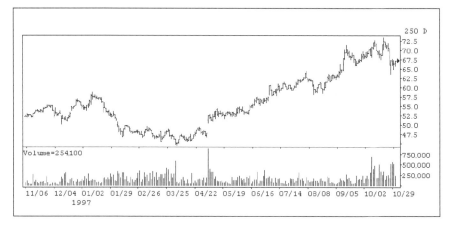

Fig 27.1 ■ Western Atlas

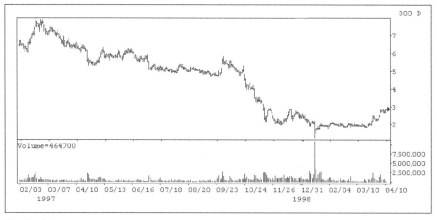

Fig 27.2 ■ Echo Bay Mines

Now combine a selling frenzy with a negative recommendation from your broker to find another stock to watch for the future

Figure 27.2 shows the January 1998 final price drop in Echo Bay Mines on extremely high volume. Note that the single price bar has a very big range relative to all of the bars that preceded it. While the market did not reverse at that time, the supply of stock had finally been exhausted and prices stabilized.

This stock has found its bottom. Selling here would be too late to rescue any additional capital even though the fundamentals still looked very bad. Of course, this does not tell you that the stock will reverse course and go up but you can be confident that you have time to find a better place for your money without panicking.

Breakout warning

Stocks and markets can trade in flat, tight ranges on low volume for weeks, if not months. When volume suddenly spikes up but price does not move, a warning is flashed. A small number of participants have suddenly taken an interest in the stock and this is shown by the volume increase. However, since information flows are far from perfect, the majority of market players do not follow this lead and therefore do not push up price. Eventually, the 'herd' discovers this activity and the reasons behind it, whether they be fact or rumour, and start to take notice. The stock then breaks out of its range.

Figure 27.3 shows Charming Shoppes in a small flat range in mid-1997. On 27 June, volume spikes but the stock was unchanged for the day. Two trading days later, the market woke up, broke out of its range and began a 12-week rally.

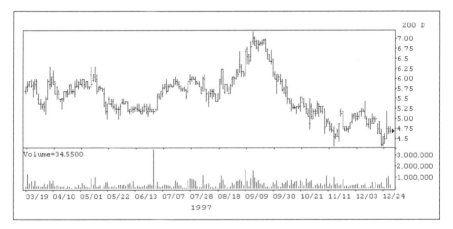

Fig 27.3 ■ **Charming Shoppes**

Confirmation required

Not all volume spikes have lasting technical meaning. In the stock market, dividend capture strategies, legal insider activities, options expirations and changes to indices often lead to high volume days. Futures markets also can have spikes during expirations and rollover periods. First Union Corp volume spiked higher in September 1997 but did not set a new rally high, break from a trading range or technical pattern (Figure 27.4). In this case, it was the result of a pending joint venture.

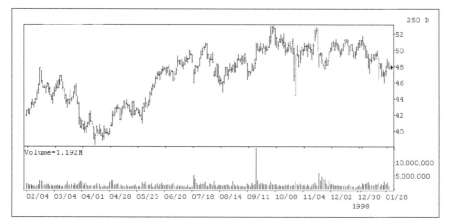

Fig 27.4 ■ First Union

The bottom line is that volume spikes have different meanings depending on where they are in the charts. They should be used as warnings and confirmations and not as buy or sell signals by themselves.

If your broker has a stock on the list for you, and there is no clear bullish indication in trend or divergence in an indicator, watch for volume. It is usually a leading or coincident event, and rarely lags a technical breakout.

What makes a stock look good?

This was covered in Chapter 14. If stocks from the list meet these criteria, then you have a very good starting point.

Compare it to the market

If your broker's picks do pass these first tests, the next step is to compare them to their sectors and their sectors to the market. Rather than rehash relative strength analysis here, turn back to page 139 to review this concept. Substitute your stock and its group once you have analyzed the group to the market.

Compare them to each other

You have now narrowed the broker list to just a few candidates that have met the criteria outlined at the beginning of the chapter. Run relative strength tests on this small group, one stock against another, until you see a very select group. Chances are, the combination of good fundamentals and good technicals will be powerful for this group and they will all fire well. However, your investment capital is not unlimited so you want to choose the best of the best.

Congratulations! you have just selected stocks in the same way as almost all mutual fund managers.

part

6

Further on down the road

Stop!

The next few chapters deal with confusing issues that you do not need to know right now. Feel free to peek but do not be intimidated. There is no test and you do not need to learn these topics just yet.

28 Introduction to candlesticks

Except for the chapters involved with simplifying the data in the chart to make the major trends jump out, this book has not covered much about the actual presentation of the price data. Most of the charts used in Europe and the Americas are daily bar charts. These were simplified by using line charts or weekly and monthly charts. In the Eastern countries, a technique known as candle charting is a very widely used method and it deserves a special mention here. That it is gaining in popularity in the West makes it more compelling.

Candle charts, or candlesticks, use the same data as bar charts but they emphasize the open and the close, rather than the high and the low. For those interested in details and history, there are several good references to provide an explanation. This is just a brief outline. Almost all of the commercial charting packages and software include candlesticks for you to use when you are ready to try them.

Over 100 years before traditional bar and point and figure analysis originated, the Japanese were using their own style of technical charting that would eventually evolve into the candlestick techniques currently in use today. Many candlestick patterns are similar to those of western technical analysis but they have several advantages. One is their descriptive names. For example, the equivalent of a bearish one-day reversal, one where price gaps higher on the open, continues to make new highs but changes course to end up closing lower, is called a 'dark-cloud cover'. As its name implies, the market is about to get stormy and investors should make preparations (i.e. sell).

Candlestick charting offers unique advantages.

While it is important to view the markets as other participants do, candlestick charting offers other unique advantages. One important advantage comes from the combining of patterns. These often reveal changes in volatility and momentum without the use of oscillators and other derivatives of price. By using oscillators in addition to candlesticks, the analysis becomes very powerful.

Reading candlesticks

Like a bar chart, the daily candlestick line contains the open, high, low and close for the market on a specific day. However, unlike a bar, the candlestick has a wide part that is called the 'real body'. It represents the range between the open and close. When the real body is black (i.e. filled in) it means the close was lower than the open. If the real body is white (i.e. empty), it means the close was higher than the open. See the candlestick illustrations in Figure 28.1.

The thin lines above and below the real body, which resemble the wicks of the candle, are called the 'shadows'. The shadows represent the high and low of the day. The shorter the upper shadow on a black body, the closer the open was to the high. A short upper shadow on a white body means that the close was near the high. The relationship between the day's open, high, low and close determine the look of the daily candlestick. Real bodies can be long or short and black or white. Shadows can be long or short as well.

Basic candlestick shapes

Long black body – this represents a bearish period in the market. Prices experienced a wide range, the market opened near the high and closed near the low of the period.

Long white body – this is the opposite of a long black body, and represents a bullish period in the market. Again, prices experienced a wide range, however, the market opened near the low and closed near the high of the trading period.

Spinning tops – these are small real bodies, and can be either black or white. The small body represents a relatively tight range between the open and close for the period. In a trading range environment, spinning tops are neutral, but they may become important parts of other chart patterns.

Doji lines – pronounced 'doh jee', These illustrate periods where the opening and closing prices for the period are the same. The length of the shadows can vary. Doji lines are important in a variety of patterns.

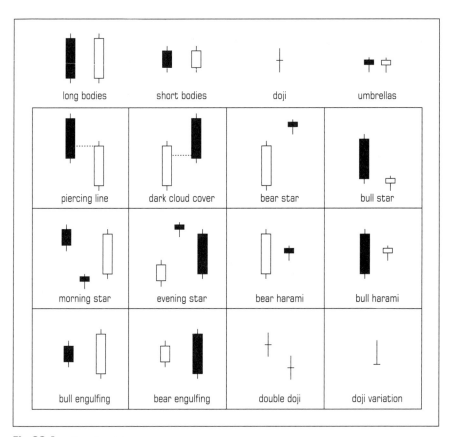

Fig 28.1 ■ Candlesticks

Reversal indicators

As with Western analysis, candlesticks can forecast changes in market direction. Some have only one candle, usually with a specific shape. Others have two or more candles combining simple candles into more exotic shapes.

The simplest reversal pattern is the *umbrella* candlestick. It gets its name from its somewhat remote resemblance to a rain umbrella. However, it can be more objectively recognized by two features: 1) a spinning top real body at the upper end of the entire trading range, with little or no upper shadow, and 2) a lower shadow that is at least twice the length of the real body. The colour of the real body is not important.

Umbrellas can be either bullish or bearish depending on where they appear in a trend. If they occur during a downtrend, they are called *hammers* and are bullish, as in 'the market is "hammering out" a base'. If an umbrella appears in an uptrend it is bearish, and is referred to as a *hanging man*. The latter's ominous name is derived from its look of a hanging man with dangling legs.

The *engulfing pattern* is a strong reversal signal, especially after a prolonged trend. It is similar to the Western reversal pattern. Only the real body is important in this formation; shadows are virtually ignored.

The bearish engulfing pattern has a black real body that engulfs the prior day's white real body. In other words, during an uptrend, the market gapped higher and closed lower than the previous day's close. Conversely, a white body at the bottom of a downtrend that engulfs the prior day's black body is a potentially bullish signal.

The *piercing line* is a bullish pattern. This combination is composed of a long black body followed by a white body after a market decline. The white body should open lower and then close above the centre of the black body. Here, the market gaps lower on the opening and then retraces to close above the midpoint of the previous period's black body. If the white body does not 'pierce' this halfway point, more weakness can be expected in the market.

As mentioned earlier, the *dark cloud cover* is a bearish pattern. This is the opposite of a piercing line. A strong white body is immediately followed by a black body after a rally. A dark cloud cover must have a black body opening above the high of the previous white body as well as closing below the white body's centre.

There are various candle combinations called *stars*, so named because they are located significantly above their preceding candles like a star in the sky. All stars are reversal indicators and are more important after prolonged trends or large moves. A star is a small real body or a doji made on a gap that follows a long real body. Even if the shadows overlap, the formation is still considered a star, since only the real bodies are important.

The *morning star* pattern is a signal of a potential bottom in the market. It is aptly called a morning star because it appears just before the sun rises (in the form of higher prices). After a long black body, there is a downside gap to a small real body. This is followed by a white body that closes above the midpoint of the black body made just before the star. The morning star is similar to a piercing line with a 'star' in the middle.

The *evening star* formation is the reverse of the morning star. Aptly named because it appears just before darkness sets in, the evening star is a bearish signal. The evening star is similar to a dark cloud cover with a 'star' in the middle.

The *doji star* appears after a prolonged move, and is composed of a gap and a doji line (remember a doji is when the open and the close are the same price). It is the same as an evening or morning star but with a doji in the middle. This is often the sign of an impending top or bottom. Doji stars often mark imminent turning points in the market, but more conservative traders should wait for the next day's body to confirm a change in price trend.

The *shooting star* pattern appears at short-term tops in the market, and is a bearish signal. As its name suggests, the shooting star is a small real body at the lower end of the price range with a long upper shadow. Think about a shooting star streaking across the sky leaving a big smoky tail in its wake.

Harami lines are similar to an inside day in contemporary Western analysis, but while an inside day is usually considered neutral, the harami line is an indication of a waning of momentum. The small body of the harami line is contained within the long body directly preceding it. (Harami appropriately means pregnant in Japanese.) If the harami line is also a doji, it is referred to as a *harami cross*.

These patterns indicate that the market is at a point of indecision and a trend change, or a reversal, is possible. The harami cross pattern is useful in forecasting trend changes – especially after a long white body in an uptrend.

As with bar charts, most candle patterns need to be confirmed by price action after the fact.

Continuation indicators

Candle patterns can also indicate that the market will continue its current trend. There are many types that occur but for now the *window* will suffice.

A window is the same as a gap in contemporary western analysis. With bar charts, we say 'filling in the gap', the Japanese expression is *'closing the window'*. Gaps often become support or resistance areas and windows (i.e. gaps) are viewed in the same context as support or resistance. Shadows are also considered in closing the window. Unclosed windows signal continuation of the trend.

Dojis

Doji lines are important enough to get their own discussion. Basically, dojis reflect indecision, which makes sense since the market closed at its open after trading significantly higher and lower intraday. If you see two or more doji lines within a short time in a market where this normally does not occur, then a strong move is pos- | **Dojis reflect indecision.** sible. *Double dojis* may foretell an increase in market volatility and would be of special interest to options traders.

Doji days can become support or resistance, usually on a short-term basis. A series of three doji lines after a prolonged move could signal a rare and important top or bottom.

Variations on doji patterns have interesting names like rickshaw man (very long shadows) and gravestone (no lower shadow and a very long upper shadow). However, their significance remains the same as other dojis.

Trading with candlesticks

Now put some of the basic candle formations to work, with other technical indicators, to analyze a real market situation.

Figure 28.2 shows cocoa futures from April to June 1992. The biggest question a trader would ask during this period is 'When will this market stop going down?' There are several patterns on the chart that forecasted times for corrections and finally, the end of the decline. Using candlesticks with other confirming technical indicators lets you figure out which is which.

1. The market was trending lower and at the bottom of the channel. The gap lower (called a window) could have signalled a continuation of the decline on a bar chart. The candle after the gap had a small real body (the wide part of the candle marking the open and close). This is known as a star and signifies uncertainty in the market. The next day the market opened higher and closed within the real body of the candle before the gap. This completed what appeared to be a morning star and would be a bullish reversal pattern.

2. But was that the bottom of the decline? First, the white candle did not close above the mid-point of the first black candle. The three spinning tops that followed indicated that the market did not really have much buying support so the channel was not broken.

3. At the channel bottom, the one-day reversal pattern on a bar chart appeared as an engulfing line with candlesticks. The white real body 'engulfs' the previous black real body.

4. Here a doji, which has no bar chart equivalent, signifies that the rally again did not have sufficient buying power. The market opened and closed at the same price after trading in a wide range. Dojis are very good at calling market tops. The next day, cocoa gapped up at the open and then proceeded to fall until it closed virtually unchanged (the long black body is bearish).

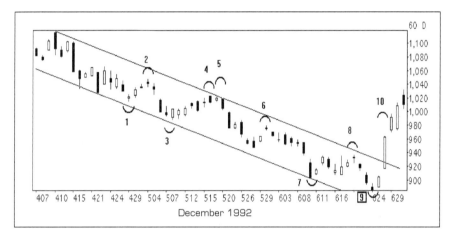

Fig 28.2 ■ Cocoa futures

5. Further confirmation was found with the small candle the next day (uncertainty) and another long black body, which failed to break the channel. The small real body completely within the larger real body of the previous day, a reversal indicator, is a harami and forcasted a trend change.

6. Things were starting to look good again until the star said otherwise. This pattern was completed the next day with the gap lower to a black body, this time resembling an evening star. This particular evening star was not as perfect as the trader might like because the last candle should really close within the real body of the candle preceding the gap up. (A check of the then-current month, July, shows a better pattern.)

7. Once again, at the bottom of the channel, a harami.

8. Once again, at the top of the channel, a doji.

9. This morning star is much stronger as the final white candle is long and closes well within the first black candle. Add to this the fact that prices did not make it back to the bottom of the channel this time and that the RSI bottomed out at an oversold level at No. 7, there is confirmation. This is the true bottom.

10. Very strong white candle breaks through the channel.

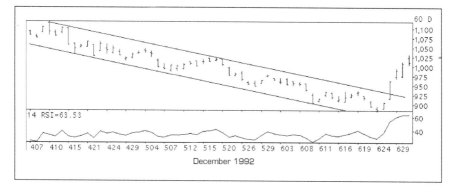

Fig 28.3 ■ Cocoa futures-bar

Figure 28.3 shows the same market but as a bar chart. First, note the RSI divergence as mentioned above. Next, notice that on 25 June, the date that the morning star completed, there was no bullish indication. The bar chart trader would have waited until the trend break and missed out on about 30 points!

Cycles

Most technical analysts study price movements using bar charts. This method, while very important, does not take advantage of the 'other' data series on the chart, time. (Although point and figure and tick volume charts are used to study price movements without regard to time at all.) Cycle analysis attempts to find recurring major and minor peaks and troughs in price movement for better trade timing. This chapter will take a brief look at cycles and highlight a particular use.

> Cycle analysis attempts to find recurring major and minor peaks and troughs in price movement for better trade timing.

What is a cycle?

A cycle is a regularly occurring sequence of events. The sun rising every morning and setting in the evening is a cycle. The four seasons are one cycle. In financial and commodity markets, a cycle is loosely defined as price movement of a market from a local bottom to a local top and back again. For example, a stock's natural ups and downs may come at regular three-month periods. Every three months, falling prices tend to make a local bottom. In between the bottoms, rising prices tend to make a local top. Knowing where these reversals tend to occur can help time purchases at cycle bottoms and sells at cycle tops.

Cycles, just like price trends, can be long, short or intermediate in length. A specific market may have a 20-day, 52-week and 5-year cycle, all acting together to describe price activity. By adding the cycles together, the actual price activity can be forecast.

To better illustrate how cycles are added return to the example of the sun and the seasons. By adding the annual seasons cycle to the daily sun cycle, you can forecast a likely temperature for any time of day for any given date (Figure 29.1).

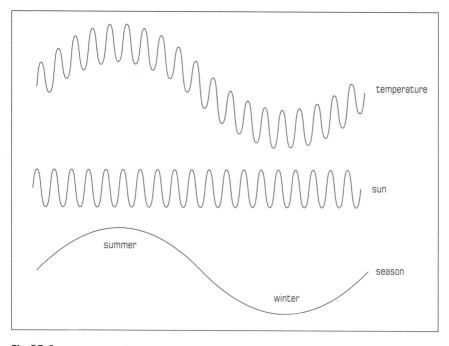

Fig 29.1 ■ Cycles

US treasury bonds showed very clear cyclical behaviour in the mid-1980s (Figure 29.2). From the major low in mid-1984 to the major low in 1987, both marked with 'M', you can deduce a rough three-year cycle. (One pair of major lows does not define a market's cycles. Here a longer-term chart does confirm a slightly longer than three-year cycle.) Within the long-term cycle, there is a medium-term cycle of about eight months in length. Each of these minor cycle bottoms is market with an 'm'. Just as in the previous weather example, adding the two cycles together defines the likely trading activity in the market. A shorter-term chart would also show daily and intraday cycles to further refine the market forecast.

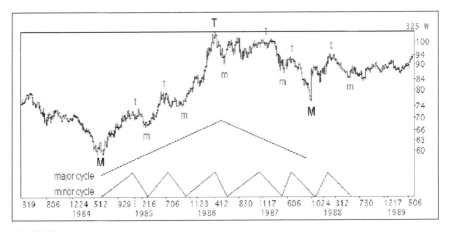

Fig 29.2 ■ **US T-bonds**

Left and right translation

In a trading range, cycles are fairly regular in that the market peaks halfway through the cycle. However, when a market is trending, the cycle peak tends to shift left or right in the direction of the larger trend. This is consistent with the notion that in rising markets, prices should spend more time going up and in falling markets, prices should spend more time going down.

For example, in the bond example above each of the intermediate peaks (labeled 't' for top) between the major bottom in 1984 and the major top ('T') is shifted to the right. After the market starts to decline, the one clear peak is shifted to the left. During the transition period from major bull to major bear market, bonds traded in a volatile range and the peaks were more centred.

Profiting

In a flat market, such as the period from October 1993 to February 1994 in bonds (Figure 29.3), the daily chart of bonds illustrates a short-term three-week cycle. Each cycle bottom occurred on or near support at 113. Buying bonds at the cycle low and reversing the position 1½ weeks later proved to be a successful low-risk strategy.

The cycle peaks were in the middle of the cycle (no translation) since the larger market trend was flat. Note that the late January cycle bottom never really made it to the support line, which reinforces the need to use several technical indicators for trading. A trader using support and resistance levels alone would have missed the opportunity.

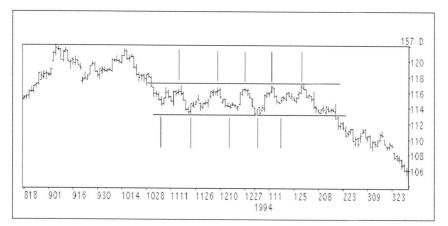

Fig 29.3 ■ US T-bonds later

In a rising market, such as that in Figure 29.2, the intermediate cycle tops provided good places to take profits ahead of each intermediate correction. Conversely, when the major cycle was in a declining phase, the minor cycle bottoms provided good places to take profits from short positions. Again, they were not good places to buy since the trend was down.

Summary

This has been an overview presentation of how cycles interact to define markets and there is much that has not been covered here. In the real world of trading, the size (price moves) and the frequency (cycle lengths) can vary from cycle to cycle in the same market. Cycle analysis is a tool to be used to help forecast *likely* turning points in the market and never to try to define the market specifically. The market must be allowed to tell you what it wants to do. Any other strategy is a losing proposition.

30 Technical terms you may have heard

This Chapter is a brief outline of the other terms you may have heard used in conjunction with technical analysis. Do you need to know them? Not now. Consider this a quick reference guide.

Open interest

Open interest is simply the number of outstanding futures (or options) contracts for a particular commodity. In the futures markets, when one trader buys a futures contract, another trader necessarily sells one contract. In this so-called 'zero sum game', for every winner there is a loser. When the stock market crashed in 1987, many traders who bought stock index futures were bankrupted. However, these traders had to have bought their positions from somebody and those sellers collectively made a fortune. Only when a buyer later sells his position to someone who had sold short does open interest decline.

Since it takes one bull and one bear to complete a trade and increase open interest it follows that there is a conflict of opinion as to whether the market is going to go higher or lower. The more bulls and bears in the market, the higher the open interest and the more conflict there is. When prices change, one of these two groups is going to get hurt. When prices go up, the bears suffer. When prices go down, the bulls suffer.

Bollinger Bands

Bollinger Bands, also known as standard deviation envelopes, were developed by John Bollinger. Bollinger theorized that the width of an envelope should be determined by the market rather than by the assumptions of the analyst, as done with other types of trading bands and envelopes. His theory states that a trading envelope's distance from the mean is a function of the market's volatility. This makes sense because a volatile market does have wider swings from its average, even though a distinct trend may be in effect. The bands should expand to account for this, rather than be subject to

> When a market is flat, the bands should tighten so that a breakout can be signalled early.

giving false reversal signals. Conversely, when a market is flat, the bands should tighten so that a breakout can be signalled early.

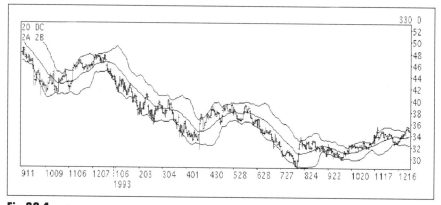

Fig 30.1 ■ Merck with Bollinger bands

Figure 30.1 is a daily chart of Merck with Bollinger bands added. Bollinger recommends that each band be shifted two standard deviations from the average so prices remain within the bands about 85 per cent of the time. When prices move outside the bands, the following analysis can be applied.

Sharp moves after a relatively calm market tend to occur after the bands tighten to the average (volatility lessens). In November 1993 the bands became quite narrow and that was followed by a quick three-point move.

The reason for this is that market participants have slowed their activities and are waiting for the market to tell them where it is heading. Once a move starts, everybody jumps in to trade it.

A move outside the bands calls for a continuation of the trend, not an end to it. Often, the first push of a major move will carry prices outside of the bands. This is an indication of strength in an up market and weakness in a down market. This can be seen nearly everywhere on the chart.

This is because volatility has not expanded yet to compensate for the new trend. Other indicators, such as RSI, can confirm this.

Bottoms (tops) made outside the bands followed by bottoms (tops) made inside the bands call for reversals in trends. Note how Merck made a new high in December 1992 outside the bands while the next price peak occurred inside the bands.

This is because market participants have not accepted the increase in volatility and therefore look for wide price swings to take profits.

As mentioned, a 20-period average with two standard deviations is commonly used. However, Bollinger points out that the interval one is analyzing may require longer or shorter average and deviation calculations. For example, analysts trying to gain perspectives on longer-term periods may find 50-day averages with 2.5 standard deviation bands optimal. Conversely, those studying short-term intervals may find 10-day averages with 1.5 or 1.0 standard deviations more interpretive.

Relative Strength Index (RSI)

The Relative Strength Index (RSI) was developed by J Welles Wilder, Jr. As a momentum indicator, the RSI measures the velocity of price movements. In this model, prices are generally considered to be elastic in that they can move only so far from a mean price before reacting or retracing. Rapid price advances result in overbought situations and rapid price declines result in oversold situations. The slope and values of the RSI are directly proportional to the velocity and magnitude of the price move and are extremely helpful in identifying overbought and oversold situations.

The core of the formula for RSI takes the last 'n' periods and divides the gross positive changes per period by the gross negative changes. This means that the more often prices move higher in that 'n' period span and the greater those changes become, the higher the RSI value. By depending on both the number of up closes and the magnitude of those closes, RSI filters out normal volatility difference between markets while maintaining the significance of single large price moves. By reducing the number of periods in the calculation, RSI can be made more sensitive (faster).

The RSI value itself ranges from 0 to 100 and support, resistance and market trends can be found on the RSI plot. Generally speaking, an RSI value above 75 indicates a possible overbought situation and a value below 25 indicates a possible oversold situation. This does not mean, however, that a market will immediately reverse once either of these levels is reached. It is more likely that the market will pause to consolidate, resulting in a more neutral RSI value. The RSI chart is most often used in conjunction with a bar chart. Relatively high RSIs (55–75) normally accompany a positive price trend and relatively low RSIs (25–45) normally accompany a negative price trend. Divergences between price action and the RSI plot could signal market reversals. See Figure 30.2 for a chart of RSI.

Stochastics

The Stochastic indicator, developed by George Lane, can be a valuable tool for identifying near-term tops and bottoms to help in timing trades closer to local reversal points. It measures the placement of a current price within a recent trading range under the theory that as a market rises, close prices tend to occur nearer to the high end of their recent range. When prices trend higher and closes begin to sag within the range, it signals internal market weakness.

Stochastics is one of a few indicators that uses two lines, known as the K and D lines (sometimes known as %K and %D). The D line is simply a smoothed version of the K and the two of them are analyzed for both overbought and oversold situations just like RSI. Two lines give the added dimension of crossovers, which are similar to price crossovers of moving averages. Stochastics is often smoothed a second time by renaming the D line to the Slow K line and smoothing it again to create the Slow D. See Figure 30.3 for a chart of Stochastics.

RSI vs Stochastics

Simply stated, the RSI yields the most meaningful results in trending markets while Stochastics works best in flat or choppy markets. While the goal of each is similar, they need to be used in different market situations. The RSI, as mentioned, helps determine when a price has moved too far too fast. This implies a trending market. Stochastics helps determine when a price has moved to the top or bottom of a trading range, which implies a non-trending (flat or choppy) market.

> RSI yields the most meaningful results in trending markets while Stochastics works best in flat or choppy markets.

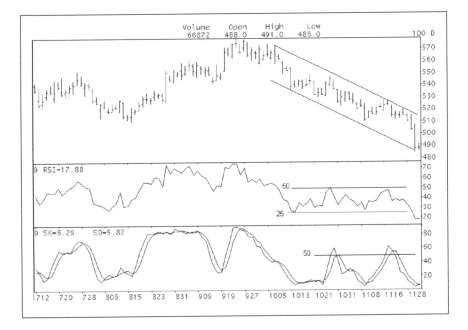

Fig 30.2 ■ Silver

Figure 30.2 shows 100 days of daily trading for the silver market with 9-day RSI and 9-day Slow Stochastics. Note how RSIs remained between 40 and 25 for most of the fourth quarter decline, never reaching the neutral 50 mark. Stochastics oscillated from a bullish 60 to an oversold 5 giving false indications of a market reversal. RSI was effective because the instrument is trending.

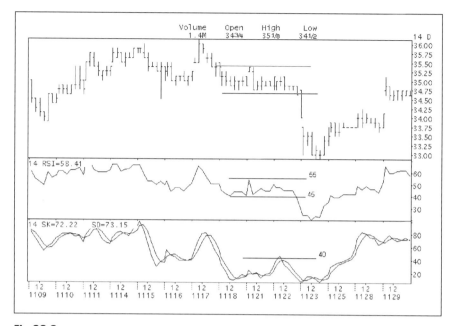

Fig 30.3 ■ Time-Warner

Figure 30.3 shows 14 days of hourly trading for Time-Warner Inc with 14-day RSI and Slow Stochastics. This stock traded in a half point range for three days. RSI values converged around the 50 mark indicating neither strength nor weakness. Stochastics, while rising for over two days, remained mostly in the bearish range under 40 and exhibited a bearish crossover early on the third day. RSIs did not indicate that the trading range had broken down until it actually happened. For a non-trending instrument, Stochastics proves more reliable.

While both RSI and Stochastics are useful in most markets, each has its own specialty. As with all technical indicators, multiple indicators give more valid signals than individual indicators.

Fibonacci retracements

Many years ago, mathematicians discovered that a certain number kept appearing throughout the natural world. It was the ratio describing how flower petals grew around their central stem, how a snail's shell swirled around its origin and how a galaxy extended from its core. For the financial community, this ratio described how consecutive numbers related to each other. This 'golden ratio' of 0.618 was applied to numbers by the thirteenth century mathematician Leonardo Fibonacci. Fibonacci numbers are really one aspect of trading with Elliot Waves and Gann Angles but those are topics for more advanced books.

The Fibonacci sequence starts like this:

1, 1, 2, 3, 5, 8, 13, 21, 34, 55, 89, 144, ...,

where any number in the sequence is equal to the sum of the preceding two numbers. The ratio of any two consecutive numbers eventually approaches 0.618.

1/1	1/2	2/3	3/5	5/8	8/13	13/21	21/34	34/55	55/89	89/144
1.0	0.50	0.667	0.60	0.625	0.615	0.619	0.618	0.618	0.618	0.618

So what does this have to do with trading? As you know, markets trend up and down, pause to retrace (consolidate, correct) then continue onward. These retracements often reclaim constant percentages of the original trend's move and can be predicted with good accuracy by Fibonacci ratios.

The ratios of consecutive numbers at the start of the sequence are 1.00, 0.50 and 0.67. Market technicians have long known that market retracements tend to end at the 50 per cent level as well as at one and two-thirds and a retracement of 100 per cent of the move provides a very strong support/resistance line. All of these are Fibonacci levels. The one- and two-thirds levels are really approximations of the Fibonacci ratio 61.8 per cent and its inverse 38.2 per cent. As you can see, Fibonacci levels are simply refined versions of what traders have been using for years.

Fig 30.4 ■ Soybeans

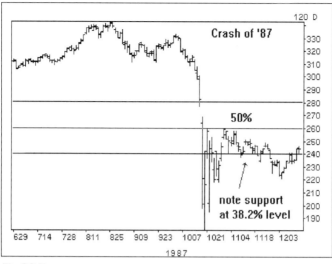

Fig 30.5 ■ S&P 500

Figure 30.4 shows the soybean market after the 1992–3 rally. Its correction ended after it lost 61.8 per cent of its gains. Figure 30.5 shows the S&P 500 after the 1987 crash. Before the year ended, the market had gained back half of its losses since the August peak. However, this level provided strong enough resistance to halt two more rally attempts.

MACD

Technical analysts often apply studies to the results of other studies; moving averages of spreads and RSIs of RSIs, to name a few. Technician Gerald Appel took a simple departure (oscillator) chart, which measures the distance between two moving averages, and overlaid a moving average of the result. This study was named Moving Average Convergence-Divergence (MACD) as it measures how two moving averages (the departure chart) move together and apart over time.

The underlying theory is that as a market moves higher, the shorter of two moving averages is above the longer average. This is because the shorter average reacts faster to price movements. The longer average will always lag behind. When the shorter average crosses below the longer, it is a signal that the trend may be reversing. Viewed in a departure chart, this crossover occurs when the two averages have the same value and therefore the spread (departure) becomes zero. Figure 30.6 shows 200 days of daily bars for the dollar/yen exchange rate with 26 and 12-day exponentially smoothed moving averages. As the market falls, the 12-day average is below the 26-day average. When the 12-day crosses above the 26-day, the departure study below crosses through zero. The departure study shows the difference between the two averages on the chart.

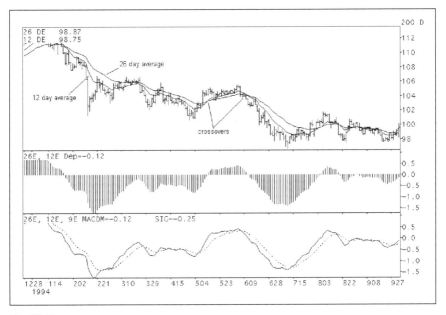

Fig 30.6 ■ Dollar/Yen

MACD starts with the departure chart and figuratively overlays a moving average of the departure values. Notice how the MACD line (solid line) has exactly the same shape as the histogram of the departure study. The dotted line is called the signal line and is just a moving average of the MACD line.

> MACD works best in a trending market or one that is trading in a volatile trading range.

Using MACD

The typical MACD analysis uses exponential moving averages. Like other momentum indicators, MACD works best in a trending market or one that is trading in a volatile trading range. In flat and quiet markets MACD can produce unreliable results.

The first indication of a change in trend is *divergence*. This is when the market makes higher highs and the MACD makes lower highs. The converse is true for falling markets where price makes lower lows and MACD makes higher lows. Figure 30.8 shows one year of daily data for cocoa futures. The divergence during the middle of 1994 is clear and the market broke its uptrend line by the third quarter of the year.

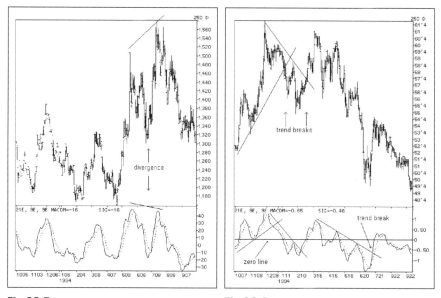

Fig 30.7 ■ Cocoa futures   **Fig 30.8** ■ Knight-Ridder

The second indication can be either a *crossover* of the MACD and signal lines, which is good for *trending markets*, or a trend break in MACD, which is good for volatile markets. The cocoa market was relatively volatile during its divergent period. Buying and selling points were indicated throughout the chart when the signal line crossed above and below the MACD line. As with moving averages and departure charts, these crossovers indicate possible entry points. Note that crossovers should occur at overbought or oversold levels of MACD. Since MACD is not indexed (like RSI or Stochastics), the definitions of overbought and oversold are market specific. For this discussion, presume that when MACD is at a relatively high level and the signal line crosses below it, a sell signal has been generated.

The next method is analyzing *trend breaks* in the MACD itself. Figure 30.9 shows one year of daily data for Knight-Ridder stock. Each trend break in MACD preceded the trend break in prices by several days. As can be seen in the July 1994 break, MACD gave a short-term signal that the bar chart did not.

When both MACD and signal lines *cross the zero line*, it is a signal that the trend reversal is complete. A market that shows divergence first, crossover or trend break second and zero line crossover third has given a very strong indication that a new trend is in force.

Introduction to Elliott waves

The Elliott wave theory was proposed in the early 1930s by RN Elliott, a stock market speculator. Elliott focused on classifying market activity according to a set of cycles and ratios of movements. As with the waves on the ocean, market activity ebbs and flows in cycles that repeat and can be subdivided into smaller cycles.

The theory states that markets move in repetitive patterns; a five-wave advance (impulse waves, labelled with numbers) and a three-wave decline (corrective waves, labelled with letters). This cycle of eight waves can be seen in all time frames from intraday to what Elliott called the 'grand supercycle' of over 200 years. Each wave in a cycle can be subdivided into smaller cycles.

Figure 30.9 shows how an eight-wave cycle advances in five waves and declines in three. One of the rising impulse waves has been broken down into five smaller waves.

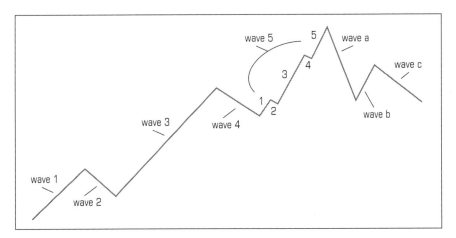

Fig 30.9 ■ Elliot waves

While the mathematics of waves and Fibonacci sequences are critical in understanding Elliott waves, the human behaviour underlying the result-ant cycles is also important. The 'personalities' of waves, as first interpreted by Elliott Wave specialist Robert Prechter, categorize why the waves rise and fall as they do.

Wave **1** includes the changing of market opinion from bearish to bullish. It often is driven by a rebound from depressed prices and is the shortest of the rising impulse waves. Basically, the bargain hunting has begun but the major-ity still is pessimistic. They just do not believe that conditions are changing.

Wave **2** is a retracement of wave **1**. Most, if not all of the gains from wave **1** are erased because market participants have used this rally to sell their losing positions at slightly better prices. This wave often presents itself as the right shoulder of a head and shoulders pattern.

Wave **3** represents when the reversal patterns completed by the first two waves break into the new trend. This is the longest and strongest of the impulse waves, at least in the financial markets, as most technical patterns have signalled the new trend and market participants now rush in to follow it. Now the crowd believes it.

Wave **4** is the consolidation phase of the advance. Its structure is also fairly complex, yielding many common continuation patterns such as triangles. This wave may never drop below the peak of wave **1**.

Wave **5** is final stage of the advance and often shows a divergence with such technical indicators as cumulative volume and the RSI. The latecomers finally climb on board.

Wave **a** at first appears to be a normal correction to the rally. Elliott theory says that wave **a** will break down into five, not three, sub-waves. A market move in five waves indicates a new dominant market direction.

Wave **b** is the bear market correction allowing a second chance for sellers to sell.

Wave **c** typically breaks support and the peak of wave **3**. Here, many technical indicators confirm that the original rally is over.

Identifying waves is often a difficult activity because there are a number of exceptions and variations in the waves.

Waves and simplicity

Reducing the noise on a chart can help in spotting wave structure. With wave analysis, you are attempting to spot the trends and counter trends in a market so that you can classify them as impulsive or corrective. Spike highs and lows as well as volatile trading patterns can hide these trends and their turning points. As seen in Figure 30.10, the rally in the Australian dollar/US dollar exchange rate began in late 1993. The wave count from the start of the move is critical in determining if it was impulsive (in the direction of the trend) or corrective. The weekly bar chart makes this a difficult endeavour.

> Reducing the noise on a chart can help in spotting wave structure.

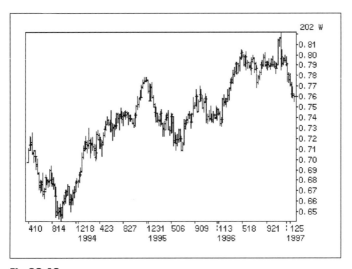

Fig 30.10 ■ Australian/US Dollar

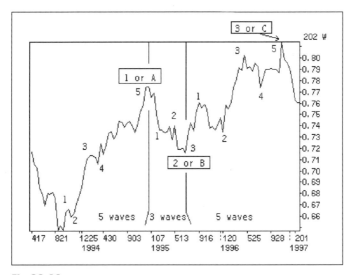

Fig 30.11 ■ Australian/US Dollar

However, a weekly line chart with a two-week interval removes enough of the market wiggles to allow you to see the wave structure clearly. The three waves highlighted are subdivided into a 5–3–5 structure. The line chart makes the minor waves jump off the chart.

Without going into the details, this can only be part of one of two patterns; a completed correction or the first three of five waves of a larger rally. Other Elliott rules need to be applied to create a forecast and the end result is not pertinent here. You can leave this topic by saying that the rising and falling trends were more readily seen with less data on the chart.

While this technique is a valuable tool, it should not be used exclusively. Not all spike highs and lows nor other wiggles should be ignored. The majority represent actual turning points in the markets but taking a step back from the data can help in seeing patterns in otherwise noisy data. Once these patterns are found, all the data are needed to make trading decisions.

Elliott waves are far too complex to be comprehensively covered here. Do not even think of using them to make your investment decisions at this time.

Tick

Rather than conjuring up images of insects or nervous disorders, the word tick is used here to describe both the minimum unit of trading (1/8 for a stock, 1/32 for a bond) and any individual trade. A ticker is simply a series of ticks (trades).

You might hear the phrase '5-tick stop'. This means that the stop price set for the trade has been set 5 ticks or trading units below the purchase price. In the US stock market, that could mean 5/8 point. Typically, the term is used for markets that trade in very small units, such as bond trading in 1/32 or 0.01 or currencies trading in 0.0001.

Another meaning for tick is as a breadth indicator for the stock market. In this context, tick is the real-time sum of all stocks whose last trade was higher than the previous trade (called an uptick) minus the sum of all stocks whose last trade was lower than its previous trade (called a downtick). This is a trading term, not an investing term so you can ignore it for now.

Trin

Trin, now known as the Arms index, is an abbreviation for trading index. It was developed by Richard Arms as a measure of volume support in the US stock market but it can be applied to any stock market around the world as long as price and volume data are available.

The formula is simple:

$$\text{Trin} = \frac{\text{number of advancing issues minus the number of declining issues}}{\text{Advancing volume minus declining volume}}$$

It seeks to measure whether advancing issues are getting their proportional share of the volume. If there are more advancing issues but more declining volume, the market is weak internally. The index would have a value greater than one in this case. Conversely, a value less than one would be bullish in that advancing issues are getting a larger share of the volume. A reading of exactly one means the relationship between advancing issues and advancing volume is in equilibrium.

Point and figure

Point and figure charting is one of the older, yet still widely used charting techniques. It is a lot more than simple jargon technicians use and cannot be given the proper treatment it deserves in a book such as this. This section will just give you a taste of this key alternative charting style.

Of the major charting styles such as bars, lines and candles, point and figure is unique in that it is constructed in a completely different way from the others but is analyzed with the same techniques. It plots price changes only, without regard to time, through a user-defined filter. This filter removes price 'wiggles' (volatility) and can be adjusted for maximum or minimum sensitivity.

Traders constructed point and figure charts by hand, before the advent of computers, partly because they could not plot each tick and continue to actively trade. By applying the filter, they only had to plot significant changes in market direction, which occur less frequently.

Chart construction

The components of the chart are the box and the reversal length. A box contains a user-designated number of change units. For example, a box size of one for CBT US Treasury Bonds would be $\frac{1}{32}$. A box size of one for the US dollar-French Franc would be 0.0001 and for Knight-Ridder stock would be $\frac{1}{8}$.

Imagine Knight-Ridder trades at 58 and then at 58 $\frac{1}{8}$. Two boxes would be plotted on the chart. If the box size were two, then only one box, encompassing both prices, would be drawn.

If prices are rising, the boxes are designated by the letter 'X'. If prices are falling, the box would then be designated by the letter 'O'. Columns of X and O are built as the market trades higher and lower, respectively. For a rising market, each time prices trade up to the next box level, an X is added to the current column of Xs. For Knight-Ridder stock with a box size of two, there would be an X at 58. When price moves up to 58¼ (two change units higher), another X would be added to the top of the column.

Since markets do not only go up, prices will eventually trade lower. A reversal occurs when prices fall by a user-defined number of boxes. For example (see Figure 30.12), if the box size is two and the reversal size is four it means that Knight-Ridder must trade lower (from the top of the column of X) by one full point. This is derived from the change unit of ⅛ times the box size of two times the reversal size of four. When a reversal occurs, a new column of letters is started to the right of the current column. In this example, a column of Os will be added.

The larger the box and the larger the reversal, the larger the filter imposed on prices. Typically, the box size is set for each specific type of instrument. For example, US stocks trading over $20 use a box size of 1 point, stocks less than that use ½ point and US treasury bonds use ½₂.

The reversal size is changed to adjust the sensitivity of the analysis. The larger the reversal, the less likely the analysis will be affected by whipsaws and volatility. The smaller the reversal, the more sensitive and detailed it will be.

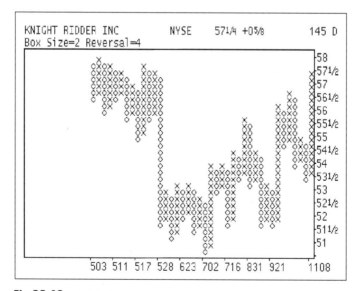

Fig 30.12 ■ Knight-Ridder

Interpreting the chart

Point and figure charts are analyzed like bar charts, using trendlines and other technical patterns. Such features as gaps are not available but the charts reveal other conditions not readily seen in bar charts. Figure 30.13 shows the February 1994 COMEX gold contract in a tick chart format. Figure 30.14 shows the same data set in a 1 by 5 point and figure chart (box=1 and reversal=5, change unit =0.1). Note that the general shapes are the same but there are two flat and wide zones at 375 and 377 in the point and figure chart. What was not readily visible in the tick chart was the fact that for two small periods of time, the market was very volatile, showing several reversals in succession. The wider the point and figure pattern, the more significant it becomes. In this case, the 375 area provided strong intraday support and the 377 area showed a strong resistance to the rally. These two zones are labelled in both charts as 'A' and 'B' respectively.

Fig 30.13 ■ Gold tick chart

Fig 30.14 ■ Gold point and figure chart

31 Debunking the TV analyst

This is where the analyst is separated from the analysis. The technician appearing on a television news show to discuss the market is most likely an experienced practitioner of technical analysis. This is probably someone who has a good track record picking stocks or trading commodities, has written a book or two and looks forward to a nice bonus from the firm at the end of the year. The bottom line is that the analyst on TV is probably good at the job.

'You looked good but I didn't understand a thing you said.'

However, being interviewed on TV is not a job. Like it or not, even the most stodgy of business television shows is more interested in ratings than in dispensing good investment advice. Of course, ratings will eventually fall if their guests are consistently wrong on the markets but their day-to-day operations depend on entertainment. The message is business but the guest who bores the audience will not be asked to return.

There are two big and often unattained goals for TV analysts. The first is that they need to be interesting. As mentioned above, the analyst may have a 100 per cent track record but if the audience cannot bear to sit through the presentation, the information is lost.

The second goal is that they need to be understood. You may enjoy the tirade one analyst makes against regulators or a class of stocks but what useful information do you really get from the show? Did the analyst leave you with a specific investment idea or even some fact you will remember?

'I'm long-term bullish.'

(Great, but what do I do *now*?)

Imagine that you have seen a stock market wrap-up show on your local news channel. Assume that the analyst made a clear prediction on the stock market and interest rates over the next few months, listed favourite stocks and tied the whole thing up in a compelling argument with connections to the economy and world events. In other words, an ideal guest on the show from both the producer's and the audience's points of view.

One week later, a deep freeze grips Europe, destroys crops and precipitates storms that severely damage the oil-drilling capacity in the North Sea. Commodity prices begin to rise and production of finished goods starts to slow due to shortages. The TV analyst just made rosy predictions for the stocks of companies that are now reeling in the wake of what can be classified a natural disaster.

Was the analyst wrong? Absolutely not. However, you, as the TV viewer, were not privy to the analyst's private market call to customers several days ago were recanting previous advice and recommending selling several sectors.

> Technical analysis deals with probabilities to help the analyst figure out how to act.

Is this simply trying to have it both ways, being bullish and bearish, to cover all the bases? Again, no. Making the first prediction, the technical and fundamental conditions in the markets were positive. Suddenly, a natural change in the weather set off a chain reaction and turned the indicators bearish.

Remember, technical analysis does not seek to predict the future. It deals with probabilities to help the analyst figure out how to act. If the market says it wants to go up, then buy. If it then changes its mind, technical analysis will allow the investor to get out soon with minimal losses.

If this example seems too complex, then just think about how the markets were changed in 1991 when Iraq attacked Kuwait. The TV analyst certainly did not plan for any actions by Iraqi military strategists but when the markets moved though technical levels, the technician was able to react quickly. Unfortunately, it did not happen on TV for everyone who saw the first broadcasts.

'They don't tell you when to sell and are therefore not accountable to you.'

Among some of the more useless comments made on television and radio and in newspapers and magazines are the following:

'I'm cautiously optimistic.'

'The easy gains have been made.'

'It's a stock picker's market.'

Consider that last one again. You have just heard a speaker who is an expert on the obvious.

Another of the more useless, if not dangerous, comments made is the fundamental rating of 'outperform'. You hear analysts rate stocks and sectors as 'outperformed' or 'overweighted'. They are trying to say that these stocks will provide better rates of return than the general market over a specified period of time. The latter term means that they are recommending that portfolios contain a higher percentage of the stock or sector than the general market contains, again because they think the stock or sector will outperform.

The trusting investor then goes in the market to buy these stocks and the market drops. The stocks he bought outperformed the market because they went down less so the analyst says he was right. The investor lost money anyway.

If a stock falls less than the general market, it has outperformed the market. Unless the analyst rates it as a 'buy' and gives price targets as well as telling us what has to happen to prove him wrong, enjoy the analyst for entertainment value only.

Summary

- The TV analyst must be interesting. Giving valid investment advice is a secondary consideration.
- The TV analyst must make sense. Even if correct, the analyst still must communicate it to you in terms you can understand.
- Do not base your trades solely on a TV show. The analyst's paying customers have access to changes in the original forecast. You do not.

Fun with jargon

Technicians use so much jargon that the subject sounds strange to normal people. Fundamentalists talk a good story because they use understandable words like sales, inventory and revenue. Technicians have terms like double bottom, dark-cloud cover and breakout. This section takes a look at a few you might have heard before or read about in other books.

Double reverse whirligig

OK, just kidding, but there are lots of fun names and descriptions technicians use to classify the markets.*

Bear trap

Trading jargon is rich with metaphors of war and death. The hunting theme fits well with all of the macho language used by even the mildest mannered analysts.

A bear trap is essentially a false breakout from a chart pattern (see Figure 1). The market breaks a support level but is not supported by other technical conditions such as volume or price momentum. Perhaps the supporting pattern border was not clear.

> Trading jargon is rich with metaphors of war and death.

Maybe the market simply drifted through the support without a significant vertical price move.

Remember, the term breakout suggests that the current pattern is broken. A crack or chip in the pattern without the market escaping from within draws in the aggressive bears, trapping them in a losing position. As soon as the market moves back within the pattern, the nimble technical analyst realizes what has happened and quickly exits the bearish position.

The same is true for the converse bull trap. A false breakout higher from a pattern draws in the bulls to trap them in a losing position. Either way, the breakouts were not strong and are quickly reversed.

---

*The name comes courtesy of Mark Leheney, News Development Manager, BridgeNews.

Fig 1 ■ Australian/US dollar

Dead-cat bounce

Animal rights activists and some mutual fund investors prefer the term dead-analyst bounce but that is another issue.

There comes a time in every bear market when even the most ardent bears re-think their positions. Value investors may think the bottom has been reached so they nibble at the market a little. Momentum players may look at their indicators and find oversold readings. The bottom line is that buying pressure awakens, even if only briefly, to send the market up off its lows.

They say that if dropped from a high enough point, even a dead cat will bounce. This translates to the financial and commodity markets surprisingly well as can be seen in Figure 2. Gold prices (weekly chart, three years) peaked in January 1996 before beginning a relentless bear market. A resisting trendline contained all major rallies since that time. The parallel channel line drawn below the market was violated to the downside in January and February of 1997 making the market outlook bleak.

However, several technical factors were present to contradict this view. First, the RSI was at its lowest levels in years. Second, a one-week reversal pattern was scored in the week of 10 February. Finally, the five to six-month cycle that could be seen over the span of the chart was at its end. The combination sent the market sharply higher in a reaction rally. Unfortunately for the bulls, the following two weeks of gains were immediately halved by an even larger downside reversal below the resisting trendline. In this case, the dead cat was dropped from a high enough point (in terms of price and time) to bounce but it was not enough to change the trend.

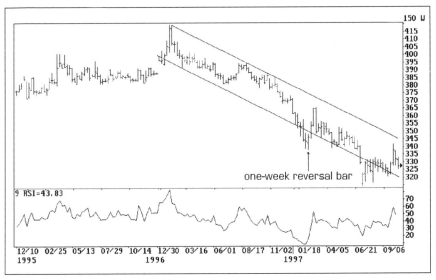

Fig 2 ■ Gold

Bounce or reversal?

Gold had a dead-cat bounce. The Nikkei 225 index in Figure 3 shows a similar price pattern in 1995 but had a bullish divergence in its RSI indicator. The price index made a lower low while RSI did not. Departure below the 52-week moving average (spread between price and moving average) was also at a relatively high level. In other words, the market had fallen far below a reasonable trend and it was about time for a change of short-term trend within the long-term trading range.

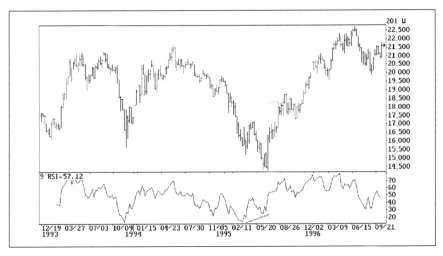

Fig 3 ■ Nikkei

Daily charts (not shown) showed a double bottom and bullish RSI divergence while several other technical factors were also positive. This confluence of bullish indicators signalled a reversal, not a bear market bounce. Here, the market then began a year-long rally that took it to the top of its long-term range.

Conclusion

The differences between a bounce and a change in trend are mostly in degree. Bounces are usually based on oversold conditions. Reversals are based in changes in market perceptions. The latter can be found in traditional chart patterns, market sentiment and supply and demand relationships. In either case, the technician can be positioned to take advantage of the initial move higher before having to decide if there really is a new trend to follow.

> The differences between a bounce and a change in trend are mostly in degree.

Whipsaw

This term may trace its origins back to a woodcutting tool but it is better to concentrate on the 'whip' part of the name.

A whipsaw is a trading signal that gets reversed immediately. How can that be? Technical signals and systems should not do that. Well, the truth is that they can. There is always that trade-off between sensitivity and risk as you want your indicators to tell you to act but you do not want them to constantly fire. If you use less sensitivity, they fire less often and you miss opportunities. If they are too sensitive, then they fire a lot, you catch every signal as well as fall victim to market noise.

There are many indicators from which to choose and some work better in certain market conditions. For example, a trend-following indicator, such as a moving average, needs a trend to follow. In a flat market, it will give many false signals.

Figure 4 shows one year of daily data for Bethleham Steel. After a multi-month decline, the stock levelled out in the 8–10 range. Both the 40-day and the 200-day moving averages flattened to indicate that in both of those two frames the market was trendless. Note that prices moved above and below the averages often to generate many false breakout signals.

Do not forget, most of us have to deal with transactions costs. Whipsaws raise the costs of achieving the same gross profit.

```
D Price                                          03/29/99
Bethlehem Steel Corp                    8 3/16       250 D
40 DC              8.41
100 DC             8.62                                    16
                                                          15
                                                          14
                                                          13
                                                          12
                                                          11
                                                          10
                                                           9
                                                           8

  04/01 05/13 06/24 08/05 09/16 10/27 12/08 01/21 03/04
                                                  99
```

Fig 4 ■ Bethlehem Steel

Catapult

A catapult is a chart pattern showing a breakout, test and strong resumption of the new trend. The market makes a tentative breakout only to fall back to the old pattern. However, it does not re-enter the pattern. The next move is a strong resumption of the new trend that began with the initial breakout. It is almost as if the market jumped on to a trampoline and is shot higher by the recoil.

The German DAX Index paused in late 1997 to correct a portion of its recent advance. A declining trendline provided resistance during this period until the end of the year when it was finally broken to the upside. Note that the market ran higher initially but fell shortly thereafter. Technicians call this a 'test' of the trend break. After the market proved that it could remain above its former resistance line, the index 'catapulted' higher to start a long and powerful rally.

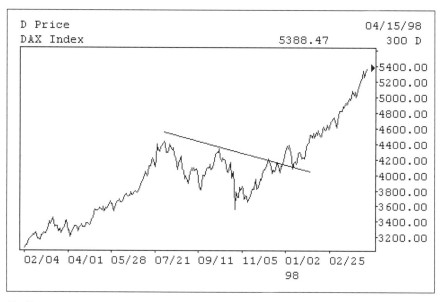

```
D Price                                         04/15/98
DAX Index                         5388.47           300 D
                                                    5400.00
                                                    5200.00
                                                    5000.00
                                                    4800.00
                                                    4600.00
                                                    4400.00
                                                    4200.00
                                                    4000.00
                                                    3800.00
                                                    3600.00
                                                    3400.00
                                                    3200.00

 02/04 04/01 05/28 07/21 09/11 11/05 01/02 02/25
                                        98
```

Fig 5 ■ A catapult

Saucers

At the ends of rallies and declines, you often look for clear reversal patterns or trend breaks. Not all rallies and declines end this way. Some involve gradual changes and slow shifts from bulls to bears or bears to bulls. Then the market slowly rolls over and begins a gradual change of direction.

A saucer pattern is also called a rounded top or bottom, depending, of course, where it forms. It is fairly difficult to detect until it is almost over since there are no clear trend breaks. It is also sometimes an exercise in subjective analysis to determine which of the many support or resistance breaks are important. The point to remember with this pattern is that the process is gradual and it will be impossible to detect the absolute top or bottom as they occur. Use saucers to confirm long-term changes in trends but not as trading signals.

Candlestick terms

There are many colourful terms from the world of candle charting. Only a selection is listed here, for entertainment value only.

Three buddhas – Resembles a large central Buddha flanked by two smaller Buddhas in a Buddhist temple. Equivalent to a head-and-shoulders.

Counter-attack lines – A strong white or black candle is followed the next day by a gap in the same direction at the open but a net unchanged price by the day's end. The first candle is the 'attack'. The second is the 'counter attack' and suggests that the tide of the battle has turned.

Dumpling bottoms – Equivalent to a rounded or saucer bottom. Dumpling tops are equivalent to rounded or saucer tops.

Tweezers – A tweezer top contains consecutive or nearby candles with the same upper shadow (daily highs). Equivalent to a double top but on a shorter-term time horizon. Tweezer bottoms have the same lower shadows (daily lows).

Upside gap two crows – The market gaps higher but closes near the low for the day. On the second day, the market opens at the same price but closes again at the low and at an unchanged level. Visualize two black crows sitting on a telephone wire and the ominous feel of this pattern is evident. It is a sign of bad luck to come.

Closing thoughts

Technical analysis is the art of science. There's a strange statement. Like psychology or sociology, it is deeply rooted in human emotions and behaviour, can be taught in an academic environment and yet cannot precisely predict what humans will do in any given situation. All of these disciplines can assess the probabilities of a response to any situation but none can be 100 per cent accurate like the 'hard sciences' of chemistry or physics.

Hard science cannot be used to predict the markets just like the square peg cannot fit into a round hole analogy. Non-linear events in the markets can only be analyzed using probabilities and technical analysis excels in just such situations. It uses past reactions to assess the probability of future actions. It also lets us know very quickly if we have misinterpreted the markets for minimum loss and maximum opportunity to find the next great trade.

This author is a firm believer in listening to the market tell him what it wants to do. The market may not care if we interpret that correctly but it will always provide us with some clues as to what we should do. Yes, we will get beaten up at times, but it is our job to survive in the game to move on to the next trade. It is also our job to listen to the market as it congratulates us when we are right. We often hear in the media that the market is 'too high'. Since when can the local talking head be right and the market be wrong? The market is always right. When we are right too, technical analysis will help us keep the winners instead of selling too soon because some human said the market is 'too high'.

Index